The Unofficial Upside Down Stranger Things Survival Guide

Nick Naughton

Contents

THE NETHER

Hugh Everett III (1930–1982) was the first physicist who proposed the many-worlds interpretation (MWI) of quantum physics - which he termed his "relative state" formulation. The theory suggests there are a very large — perhaps infinite — number of universes where parallel versions of our world might exist. The concept of a multiverse or alternate dimensions is not quite as fantastical as it sounds at first glance - though our true understanding of this field of study is still sadly and hopelessly limited to say the least.

The concept of alternate dimensions has been a staple of science fiction for many years but the general population would doubtless be astonished if they knew that parallel dimensions really did exist in reality (an alternate reality that is). It will not surprise the reader to learn though that the proven existence of a parallel dimension (which you might aptly describe as a dark echo of our own world) has been vigorously and at times ruthlessly suppressed by covert government authorities and the shadowy intelligence agencies. This is a secret that only those with the highest scientific and military security clearance have been informed about or have any awareness in regard to its existence.

Many scientists had always believed in the possible existence of dark matter alternate dimensions (or at the very least considered the concept to be plausible) so it was perhaps - to the scientific community at any rate - not quite as outlandish as it might seem when evidence for this theory finally appeared to be established and verified in 1983 (as we shall see though, it could be that intimations of the mirror realm date back ever further to 1979). It was in that year that a puzzling and nightmarish dark mirror dimension was discovered by scientists in Indiana. The discovery of this dimension was by all accounts purely accidental and proved to be highly dangerous and troublesome to put it mildly. Many lives were lost during this baffling scientific crisis.

They say you should never meddle with things you don't understand and that adage would certainly be applicable to the dark mirror dimension. The scientists in question had opened Pandora's Box but putting the lid back on proved to be a complex and dangerous task at the best of times let alone the worst. The mirror dimension proved to be a puzzle beyond our understanding and we are fortunate that the crisis was eventually quashed before it got completely out of hand and threatened the civilian population at large.

The rift or portal between our own reality and the dark mirror dimension was opened unwittingly. The scientists did not intentionally set out to find a mirror dimension but when evidence of this alternate reality began to become apparent to them it naturally became one of their main priorities - though they were still sadly engaged with other matters too which constricted their scientific exploration. The discovery of the parallel dimension was an unpredicted by-product of attempts by scientists to conduct remote viewing experiments with the aim of spying on the Soviet Union.

Remote viewing (RV) is the practice of seeking impressions about a distant or unseen subject, sensing only with the mind. The advantage of this ability is that one doesn't need to place a spy in enemy territory (with the attendant risks and complexity of such missions). The 'spy' can simply listen in on the enemy from a secure and safe location thousands of miles away. The scientific project in this case was dark indeed because there is plenty of evidence that the test subjects were being trained with a view to becoming 'remote' assassins. One can see how valuable such an ability would be to military and intelligence agencies at a time of high tension and a Cold War.

The mysterious, puzzling, and highly classified events which took place in a small Indiana town in the 1980s remain largely on a need to know basis. Documents were highly classified and in many cases shredded. Only a handful of civilians were aware of what was really happening. Some of these civilians died in the dimensional battles which took place and others survived. The one thing they had in common was that they all displayed great bravery in rising to meet the fantastical and frightening threat posed by the dark mirror world to their town. If you are to survive a dimensional crisis then you will need to be equally brave and determined and be well aware of the grave danger which will await. In the chapters that follow we shall endeavour to equip you with the information and strategies you will need if you are to have any hope of survival.

The mirror dimension was detected when a child test subject with special abilities made contact with an unknown creature in the 'void' (essentially an internal mental landscape akin to astral projection) during one of her sensory deprivation water tank Cold War remote viewing missions at the Hawkins National Laboratory. * I shall not dwell on the ethics concerning the exploitation of the test subject's powers and her general treatment - except to say that her confinement and allocated military duties would rightly not be considered acceptable for a child today. The scientists seemed to regard her as a highly dangerous weapon who needed to be kept away from the real world. This is what you might reasonably describe as a strategy at risk of becoming a self fulfilling prophecy.

The test subject at the secret laboratory had incredible abilities related to psychokinesis. Psychokinesis or telekinesis is a psychic ability allowing a person to influence a physical system without physical interaction. Little is known about the chief scientist at the lab who presided over the experiments relating to the test subject. Much of the information relating to his activities was burned and destroyed many years ago. The scientist is question was clearly (and understandably) intrigued by this remarkable (if baffling) new dimensional discovery and his scientific curiosity compelled him to investigate further. In mitigation, any scientist in his position would probably have done the same. One would feel justified in stating though that many of them would assuredly not have approved of his methods.

As a consequence of exploration, the test subject was asked to make further contact with the inexplicable and mysterious creature she had sighted in the void. Her terror at this fresh contact unleashed a tremendous surge of energy in the lab, overloaded the systems, and somehow opened a rift between our world and the mirror dimension in the form of a biological portal at the lab. As far as one can discern, this was the moment when we realised that a new field of science had been right there next to us all along. The existence of alternate dimensions was no longer merely a scientific theory of the speculative kind or pure science fiction. It was now a proven fact.

The dimensional rift which had opened appeared like a slime drenched fungus or decayed blackish vine around a lopsided doorway. In this case it was a most extraordinary doorway because it provided a passage to another dimension. The exact circumstances in which the rift opened were confined to top secret reports. It is believed that huge cracks in the lab walls began to appear before the actual portal became apparent. The human test subject generated incredible levels of energy in her terror and, as we shall discuss later, certain creatures of the mirror dimension appear to generate energy individually for the purposes of opening smaller portals. This surge of energy all somehow fused together and created a 'super portal' at the lab.

While the scientists involved in this specific mystery were intrigued and perhaps even excited by their unexpected discovery they had forgotten one important detail. They had discovered the existence of a portal to an alternate dimension but the creatures of this alternate dimension had now ALSO discovered our reality. This was decidedly not a welcome development because they were far from friendly. The entities and creatures native to the mirror dimension saw us as something to be destroyed and exterminated. They saw our reality as a place to hunt and terrify. The higher entity of this dark echo dimension wanted nothing less than to invade and conquer our world. In a worst case scenario, the scientists in Indiana had potentially placed us all in great peril and risked the end of the world. Little wonder then that they went to such great lengths to keep all of this fantastical activity a secret.

The scientists who discovered this dimension tended to refer to it as the Nether although, for reasons we shall later explain, it eventually became more commonly known as the Upside Down. Attempts by the scientists to study and explore this mirror dimension proved to near impossible. Their complete lack of knowledge concerning the mystery dimension was an obvious weakness and this strange realm turned out to be an unforgiving and coldly indifferent place of danger and despair. Hazmat suited scientists were swiftly killed when they ventured inside and instrument readings concerning the nature of this alternate reality were so unreliable they rendered any attempt to make sense of this new frontier frustratingly vague. The inhabitants of the mirror dimension did like uninvited guests. Any interloper in their reality could expect their odds of a long happy life to be considerably shortened the moment they set foot in the Nether.

The Upside Down aka Nether is a murky mist shrouded lonely dimension of gloom and despair where all is dark and decayed. One scientist was known to refer to it as the Nightmare World. Reading the data and examining the files on the Nether, one can see why. This was a Hellscape full of unfathomable bizarre science and unpredictable danger. The Nether's visual appearance is rather akin to what we would imagine a city to look like in the aftermath of a nuclear war. All is abandoned, covered in decayed roots and vines, and festooned with dirt, ash, and debris. There are signs of human life in that you'll see empty shops and ruined cars but there are no people anywhere. Only the monstrous creatures of the Nether. As we shall later see, this has given rise to nuclear theories concerning the origin of the mirror dimension.

Visibility inside the mirror dimension is very poor due to the presence of thick mist, dust, and spores. It is rather like being trapped in fog. Danger can lurk anywhere and everywhere and the poor visibility obviously makes detecting any potential danger considerably more difficult. The scientists who opened the rift soon learned that any attempt to explore this new dimension should only be undertaken with extreme caution. Your chances of survival inside the Nether will depend on how prepared you are for this decayed and grim mirror world. If you know nothing of the Nether and have no essential supplies nor a workable strategy then your chances of survival are precisely zero. The keys to your survival are your preparedness and tactics. You must maintain a high state of readiness during a Nether crisis and be able to cope with even the most extreme circumstances.

If you have the right equipment and tactics then - contrary to most available evidence - it is possible to survive the Nether but it certainly won't be easy in the slightest. There will variables that you can't account for and even the most prepared and brave person will need some luck to be on their side. Take heart though from the fact that a trip to the Nether doesn't necessarily have to be a death sentence. In the document that follows we shall discuss some of the ways in which you can survive and vanquish Nether related trouble in your vicinity. This will naturally include tips on survival in the mirror dimension.

An important thing to remind one of straight away is that a gung ho approach to Nether related trouble is not advisable. There are times when you will have to fight or go on the offensive but in order to survive you must equally use stealth, strategy, and even tactical retreats. It is intelligence that will ultimately defeat the threat of the Nether rather than brute force. The military have attempted to engage the creatures of the Nether in direct combat (most notably in 1984) but this skirmish did not go well for our dimension. Suffice to say the soldiers who took part in this limited action did not live to tell the tale.

If you find yourself in this strange and unsettling dark mirror dimension the most immediate problem you will face is the hazardous and toxic atmosphere. All scientific data collected on the mirror dimension indicates that the flora and atmosphere of the Nether is toxic and harmful to humans. You will be able to breathe but as the air is fetid and filled with dust, each hour you spend in the Nether will affect your respiratory system and make you feel progressively more sick and weak. The atmosphere inside the Nether will extract a heavy toll should one be exposed to it for an extended period. This is decidedly not a place that you want to be in for very long. Your main priority then should be to avoid this fate and spend as LITTLE time in the Nether as possible.

If you find yourself in the Upside Down, finding an exit as soon as possible is the most important thing to do but your very first task should be to find something to cover your face with. Ideally you would want a hazmat suit but this is hardly practical and something the general public are unlikely to own or get hold of easily. It is advisable to carry a scarf or a bandana as these make suitable makeshift face coverings. A medical face mask (and replacements - as face masks are small, light, and easy to store in pockets) would also be an excellent item to have on you if your town faces Upside Down trouble. The important thing is to have some sort of face mask (be it professional or improvised) so that you can restrict the amount of polluted air going into your system and lungs.

Gloves are also highly recommended in the Nether because you want your skin to touch as little as possible in the Upside Down. Another useful item to carry into the Nether would be a pair of goggles. The

Upside Down is toxic and full of spores and dust. Protecting your eyes in this environment makes very good sense. With a pair of goggles your vision will be better because you won't get dust in your eyes. With a face covering and goggles you presence in the Nether will be less taxing - though still difficult and fraught with risk. The important thing is that you'll be able to last for longer in the mirror dimension without harmful side-effects as you won't be taking so much polluted air and dust into your nose, mouth, and eyes.

The atmosphere of the Upside Down is very debilitating if one is exposed to it for a number of days. We know little about the toxins and fungi of the Upside Down but it is safe to say that exposure to these elements is not recommended. Quite the opposite. You must restrict your exposure to these elements by covering up as much of yourself as you can. Think of the environment in the event of a nuclear war. The world around you would be devastated and the air would be laden with invisible fallout danger. The Nether presents a similar sort of scenario.

There is no precise medical or scientific data concerning survival rates in the Nether but it has been calculated that a human being (one without a hazmat suit at least) would only be able to last for a matter of days before the atmosphere and toxicity became too much for them. The longest that anyone has spent inside the Nether and survived is believed to be one week. By the end of this period the person in question was seriously ill and greatly fatigued and no longer had the energy to move. When they were rescued they had been incapacitated and connected to a tentacle like tendril native to the Nether dimension. As we shall discuss later, it could be that this tendril was keeping the human (which in this case was a male child) alive for a specific purpose. Such a fate is obviously one that you should seek to avoid at all costs.

Due to the poor visibility and dense mist in the Nether it is of vital importance to use markers to trace your route if you have to venture inside this mirror world. It would be logical to - if at all possible - make these markers luminous or phosphorescent so that they may be seen clearly even in the gloom of the Upside Down. This should make sure that you don't get lost and will find it relatively easy to (should this be necessary) trace your steps back to the way you came in. This does run the risk of attracting Nether creatures but it is probably a risk you may have to take because it is of vital importance that you do not become lost in the Nether. If you end up going round in circles then you are simply going to waste much needed energy and be far less likely to find any dimensional portal.

Marker flares may also be valuable inside the Nether. In short, anything that can mark your route will be a vital mapping tool in the mirror world. To state the obvious, it would be a disaster to become lost inside the Nether. You must therefore keep track of your bearings and mark your path. One advantage is that the mirror dimension (as that term implies) appears to be a facsimile of our reality. This means that prominent landmarks or buildings in our world should also occur (that is to say be PRESENT and exist) in the mirror dimension. One can therefore use local knowledge to maintain a sense of bearings.

The buildings you are familiar with in our reality will be decayed and derelict in the Nether but they will still essentially look the same and they should be located in the same place. If you should ever find yourself inside the Nether then make use of any buildings you are familiar with to maintain a sense of your exact location. This might require a bit of exploration but even if you are transplanted to a parallel version of your home area where there are few buildings you should eventually be able to find something familiar with you can then use as a focal point in deducing where exactly you are.

Once you've done this you can attempt to draw up a logical plan for where the nearest portal might be. A government facility (which you should be able to locate if you know where you are) or the last known location of a dimension hopping Demogorgon (a Nether creature we shall discuss in depth in a later chapter) would be the most plausible locations for any portal back to our own reality. If a strange murder has occurred in your town in our own dimension then this may also lead to a dimensional rip opening. Go to the place in the Upside Down where this murder happened to check for a portal. If you stay calm and apply logical thinking to your situation (however fantastical and alarming that situation might be) then you will be able to cope much better with the awful circumstances of Nether related danger.

If you ever find yourself in the unfortunate and dangerous position of being inside the Nether then your main priority will be to find a way to get back to our own reality as quickly as possible. This is not a task that is guaranteed to be easy though. Field studies indicate that your escape from the Upside Down may well be affected by the circumstances of how you ended up here in the first place. Secret government files indicate that in 1983 a female teenager in Indiana entered the Upside Down through a tree stump portal in the woods. She thankfully managed to get back to our reality again through this portal in relatively quick time and so spent only a matter of minutes in the Nether. You must be prepared for the eventuality that you might not be so lucky as regards the amount of time you spend in the mirror dimension.

The female teenager in question was aided in escaping from the Nether by her friend pulling her back to our reality through the tree portal. She was also fortunate that the portal through which she entered the Upside Down was still open and close at hand. As we shall see, many portals do not stay open indefinitely. They are essentially like wounds in our dimension and, as any doctor will tell you, wounds eventually close and heal over time.

The female teenager is believed to have gone through the portal because she was searching for a friend who had been missing for a number of days. While you might describe her behaviour as foolhardy and not terribly sensible one can understand that she was desperate to find her friend and so seized the chance to go through the portal - despite the obvious risks and unknown factors. You may have a similar difficult decision to make should you find yourself in the middle of a dimensional crisis.

There is some vague evidence that a boy who was trapped in the Upside Down at the same time distracted a creature who was about to attack the female teenager in the Nether. The boy apparently distracted the creature with a rock - which he threw as a diversion. She was unaware of this intervention but it could well be that the boy's actions saved her life that day. She had a degree of luck that day which you can't expect to enjoy yourself. Portals between our world and the Nether vary in size and are not always consistently uniform in appearance. Sometimes they will appear to glow and pulsate - which could obviously be of assistance in trying to find one. Reports indicate that portals are sometimes reddish and usually have black roots or vines.

One common factor with mirror dimension portals is a preponderance of slime and an icky organic residue around the portal rift. Fungi like growth and tendrils may be apparent. The mirror dimension portals can be quite disgusting if one is being honest and sometimes a thick membrane will have to be broken in order for you to get through the portal barrier between our reality and the mirror dimension. You can not afford to be squeamish when it comes to the icky biological reality of portals. If you find one you will have to accept that you are liable to end up covered in slime and unpleasant Nether matter. It will be a very small price to pay though for a quick passage home to our reality.

The important thing to note is that portals do not come in one standard design. You never quite know what you are going to get or where they might appear (there has even been an instance of a portal appearing on a ceiling in a trailer park). You must quickly learn how to deduce what might be a portal. Look for a slime drenched doorway (of sorts - this doorway will obviously be of an irregular shape) or anything that appears to present an exit from the shadow dimension.

If your town experiences an Upside Down incident then you should hope that portals in the vicinity are limited in number. If there are many portals then you shall be exposed to more danger and your task will be more complex. A multitude of portals might give you more options in escaping from the Nether but this also means that more Nether creatures will be present in the vicinity and (alarmingly) our reality. The government authorities (which in this case naturally tend to be clandestine branches of the political system and highly covert) go to great lengths to contain these portals and keep their existence as secret as possible.

This secrecy is, in the case of the Nether, allegedly done in the interests of public safety. ** Those civilians who were involved in the initial Indiana incidents might regard that claim with some degree of cynicism. There is certainly evidence that the local authorities did not seem to have public safety as their overwhelming priority in the Indiana incidents we have alluded to. There is worrying evidence too that secret government agencies were prepared to kill to keep the dimensional rift a secret. Such actions obviously can't be condoned - even if the government figures in question might argue they were acting in the greater good. The safety of the public should always be the number one priority of the government.

We will discuss these matters in later chapters but you should always be aware that government agencies are to be regarded with a generous degree of suspicion in a Nether crisis. You should be wary of them and only have dealings with government figures you feel you can trust. Not all covert government officials will be obvious villains. Some of them will be decent and concerned with public safety. It is up to you (should you be placed in a situation where you have contact with a government body) to work out who can be trusted and (most importantly) who can't be trusted.

It has proven to be highly dangerous even for heavily armed soldiers and trained scientists in protective suits to enter the Nether and so the risk factor would obviously be even higher for a civilian with no military training and no protective or scientific equipment. The body count concerning the Nether and scientists and soldiers is classified and not on any official records but we suspect it might run into the dozens. The question of whether these deaths could have been avoided is beyond the scope of this document to accurately assess. Only the respective chief scientists and military officers involved in these tragic incidents would know the true answer to that.

It is therefore, given the grim statistics concerning fatalities relating to the Nether, advisable not to enter one of these dimensional portals if you can avoid doing so. The Nether is a place you must only go as a last resort. Clearly though, there are circumstances where civilians have ended up in the Nether through no fault nor intention of their own. If this happens to you one key piece of advice is not to panic. One must remain calm and clear headed. You need to be able to make logical and rational decisions and one can only do this if you remain calm. You must also conserve your energy.

If you MUST voluntarily enter the Nether (you may, for example, regard it to be the only way to save a friend and so feel that you have no choice but to enter the mirror dimension) you are advised - if possible - to do so only when you have assembled a team which has adequate protective clothing and face coverings. You should ideally make sure that your team is armed and contains members who have some weapons training and first aid knowledge. A first aid kit is also an essential - as is some water. The dangers of the Nether can never be eliminated but they can at least be mitigated somewhat with the right tactics and teamwork.

One must concede though that there is a strong possibility you may end up in the Nether alone with your colleagues left back in our own dimension. This is not ideal but it is not necessarily the end any hopes of survival. There have been lone survivors in the Nether before. You must be prepared for this scenario because during a dimensional crisis there is always a chance that it may arise and you may find yourself alone in the mirror world. There have been at least four cases where people ended up in the Nether alone. Three survived and one perished. While these are encouraging statistics one should remember that in two of these cases the survivors were only in the Nether for a matter of minutes.

It appears that finding oneself in the Upside Down is more problematic if one is zapped (for want of a better word) there in the manner that the girl test subject at the lab and the boy in Indiana were in 1983. The test subject was fortunate in that she was able to quickly locate the portal which the Demogorgon had used to enter the school (the school in OUR reality that is) in the Indiana town where all this trouble took place. She, as far as we can tell from the resulting structural damage report filed by the middle school in question, used her powers to dislodge brick and rubble - thus making the portal easier (though still not especially pleasant) to access as a means to get back to our dimension.

This was the second instance in which someone had entered the Nether but been fortunate enough to not be there for very long at all. As we have noted, it would be a mistake to assume that you might have an equally brief stay in the Nether. One would hope this is the case but you can't take it for granted that this will transpire. You must be prepared for all eventualities. It is believed the young girl with a mastery of telekinesis ended up in the Nether after vanquishing the Demogorgon in the local school. The exact circumstances of this incident remain rather fogged and are highly classified but it seems plausible to assume that she was protecting children who had sheltered her after she escaped from the laboratory.

One must concede that case studies pertaining to the lab test subject (who is classified as 011 in the secret government files which have survived) in relation to Nether related documents may not always be relevant for the simple fact that she enjoyed incredible powers of telekinesis while the vast majority of us obviously do not. Not to say though that her experiences with the Nether do not contain important lessons for us to learn. We can all seek to replicate her fortitude and bravery and there is considerable evidence that in 1985 she successfully defeated an Upside Down entity through powers of reasoning when her telekinesis had been hampered by her exposure to the Upside Down. This gives one hope that there is more than one way to survive what may appear on the surface to be a deadly and futile encounter with Nether connected antagonists.

The boy who became trapped in the mirror dimension was not so lucky when it came to swiftly escaping from the Nether. His experience in the Upside Down was considerably more complex and much longer in duration than that of others who have ended up there. He was not able to find a quick way back to our reality. This is an eventuality that you must be prepared for. If you find yourself in a similar situation you must conserve energy but still conduct a systematic search for a way out of the mirror dimension. You can rest if need be from time to time but it is vitally important to conduct a thorough exit search while you still have the necessary strength and energy to do so.

After a few days in the Nether you will find that fatigue has become a notable handicap. Your breathing will also most likely be affected by prolonged exposure to the poor air quality. As regards the former it may be advisable to carry at least one glucose drink with you in case your stay lasts longer than you expected. Anything that will provide an energy boost would be welcome. Save this drink though for when you might really need it.

It would make sense in the event of an Upside Down incident in your town to keep a log of any portals you are aware of and mark where these portals are located on a map. Make more than one copy of this map and make sure that you distribute this map among trusted colleagues. Knowing the location of each portal may come in handy even if one is trapped in the Upside Down. Because the mirror dimension apparently conforms to the geography of our reality then this map could literally be your ticket home. There is one word of warning though. The mirror dimension in Indiana conformed to the real town but we can't completely know for sure if this phenomenon applies to the rest of the United States and other nations.

All of our research indicates that it does and SHOULD do but one can never be completely sure what the rules of the Nether truly are. There is no handbook which stipulates the precise rules and nature of the Nether. All we can do is suggest theories and strategies according to the limited amount of science we DO know in relation to the mirror dimension. The considered scientific view though, based on available research, is that the Nether should correspond to the vicinity in our reality in which you entered the mirror dimension. It should be the same place but simply all decayed, dank, misty, and dangerous. A ruined and fog bound version of what you know.

There is a theory that the mirror dimension is a pocket universe and relates only to the specific place in Indiana where the initial rift was opened. Scientific journals on such matters can be dry and confusing for the layman. I therefore quote Annex fandom - 'A pocket universe or bubble universe is a concept in inflationary theory proposed by Alan Guth. It defines a realm like the one that contains the observable universe as only one of many inflationary zones. Astrophysicist Jean-Luc Lehners, of the Princeton Center for Theoretical Science, has argued that an inflationary universe does produce pockets. In his 2012 journal, Lehners wrote about how pocket universes can emerge as a result of eternal inflation.

'The mechanisms of inflation within these pocket universes could function in a variety of manner, such as slow-roll inflation, undergoing cycles of cosmological evolution, or resembling of the Galilean genesis or other "emergent" universe scenarios. Lehners goes on to discuss which one of these types of universes we live in, and how that is dependent on the measurement of the regulation of infinities inherent in eternal inflation. But, Lehners continues, "the current leading measure proposals—namely, the global light-cone cutoff and its local counterpart, the causal diamond measure—as well as closely related proposals, all predict that we should live in a pocket universe that starts out with a small Hubble rate, thus favoring emergent and cyclic models." Lehners adds, "Pocket universes which undergo cycles are further preferred, because they produce habitable conditions repeatedly inside each pocket.'"

The truth is that we simply don't know for sure what the precise rules of the Nether are in regards to its consistent predictability. If, for example, you opened a rift to the mirror dimension in a small town in Poland would that dimension mimic the real small town in Poland in the same way that the dimension in Hawkins did? It would appear more than likely that it would but it can't be completely taken for granted. You must be prepared for this possibility but if the rules of the Nether apply elsewhere as they did in Indiana then your map will be essential.

As far as we can ascertain, local knowledge should be your friend in the event of an Upside Down related incident in your town. The Nether will be frightening, dark, and hostile but it should be familiar too and this at least is one small crumb of comfort should you ever find yourself trapped there. As far as we know and according to all available evidence, guns continue to work fine in the Upside Down. There have been reported incidents of soldiers using firearms in the Nether (or at the very least tunnels which spread out from the Nether) and these weapons all functioned as one might expect in our dimension.

Whether or not these guns had any significant effect on the creatures of the Nether is another matter though and something we shall discuss in more depth in later chapters (the natives of the mirror dimension are nothing if not resilient and seem to have a high tolerance for withstanding human weapons). If you have a gun on you in the Nether it should work fine. Make sure you do not keep the gun too exposed to the elements though because the damp and dust of the Nether may cause some damage over time if you become trapped in the mirror dimension for an extended period.

Though the air is hazardous in the Nether the atmosphere is not heavy and does not hinder or constrict movement. You should be able to move freely - unless of course you are inside a hazmat suit (which is a wise health precaution but obviously a constrictive one too). The Nether is considerably colder than our world so it advisable to wear warm clothes if you are planning to venture into this dimension. The mist which seems to reside in the Nether is most likely ash and dust. You will most likely be caked in this ash after a prolonged exposure to the Nether.

If you have any spare water and are trapped in the Nether for longer than expected it might be advisable to use a small amount of water to rinse your face occasionally. If your face coverings are of the makeshift variety then you should shake these out from time to time to give rid of excess Nether dust. Try not to breathe in while you are doing this though as your face will obviously be uncovered for a moment. We have no scientific data in relation to the composition of this dust but it is probably safe to say that breathing in too much of it is not a very good idea.

If you find yourself inside the Nether it is paramount that you stay fully alert and watch everything around you carefully at all times. Make sure you remain aware of any movement on both flanks and behind you. Creatures native to the mirror dimension may be lurking nearby - most notably Demogorgons. Demogorgons are excellent at hunting and will undoubtedly stalk you if they become aware of your presence. Listen carefully for any sounds (Demogorgons are alleged to emit a clicking noise when they are very close to intended prey and they growl too if eyewitness testimonies are to be believed) and look out for any sign of suspicious movement. You must not let your concentration lapse for a single moment. Your very life will depend on your ability to do this. Stay alert and pin sharp at all times.

There have been alarming reports of incidents where the plants of the Nether have emitted a toxic substance which rendered a human being unconscious. On one occasion a victim of this toxic pollen vomited upon waking up. This is another salient reason why having face and eye protection is of vital importance in the Nether. Case studies indicate that you could survive a few hours or perhaps a day in the Nether without a protective suit and have no major ill health as

a consequence but if you spent several days inside the mirror
dimension this would not be the case and you would fall seriously
ill. The foul and dust laden air of the alternate dimension will
eventually extract a heavy toll. Breathing will become a struggle and
fatigue will set in.

The Nether mostly appears to conform to our own chronology in that
if you return from the mirror dimension you will find that same
amount of time has passed in our reality. Scientists in Indiana
initially developed a theory that the Nether existed in a different time
zone but many argue this doesn't appear to be the case and that the
theory should now not be considered to have any scientific
credibility - though advocates for this theory may disagree with that
assessment.

Suffice to say, evidence for the time dilation theory concerning the
Nether is complex. Attempts to study this theory are obviously rather
hamstrung by the limited amount of data that has been collected in
relation to how the Nether works and what the true nature of its
relationship to our reality actually is. We will later discuss a mirror
dimension entity who appeared to have the ability to manipulate time
(and thus potentially make us revise general assumptions about time
and its relationship to both realities).

Your priority - should you find yourself in the Nether - is to stay safe
and make efficient use of the time when you are still healthy and
have normal reserves of energy that will allow you to make good
progress and maintain a high degree of concentration. Do not stop
looking for an exit portal and only rest (rest is of course important)
when you deem it necessary. Do not run in the Nether because this
will only waste valuable energy and make you more easy to notice.
If you run in the Nether you are more likely to be detected and you
will also be more likely to make too much noise. This will
potentially attract predators.

Be aware that the ground in the Nether will most likely be clogged
with vines, strange roots, and creepers so the chances of tripping or
falling are higher than they would be in our reality. You must be
very conscious of this because were you to sprain an ankle or suffer
a serious foot injury your chances of finding a portal or surviving

any hostile encounter in the Nether would be considerably lessened
and nigh on impossible. The last thing you'd want is to be trapped in
the Nether with an injury that greatly restricted any movement. I am
afraid to say that if you lose the ability to walk or move then your
chances of escaping from the Nether under your own steam are
reduced to zero.

Stealth is obviously an important asset in the Nether. We shall
discuss stealth and hiding tactics later in the book in more depth but
you must obviously be as inconspicuous as possible in the Nether.
Be as silent as you can and tread very carefully and lightly. If you
have a gun only use it if you have an obvious target and feel you
have no other option but to shoot. If you fire your gun needlessly and
pointlessly in the Nether you are only going to attract unwanted
attention to yourself and you are going to waste bullets too.

Given that guns only seem to have limited effect on Demogorgons
(the primary foot soldiers of the Nether) it would be foolish to
needlessly go on the offensive in the false expectation that your
bullets are actually going to fell the creature. One should focus much
more on becoming invisible in the Nether. You do not want any of
the creatures native to this nightmare realm to know you are there.
This will not be easy but it can be done with the right tactics and
sufficient concentration. The dense mist which makes up the
unsettling aura of the mirror dimension can be used to your
advantage. Move in places where the mist is the thickest.

It could be the case that some of the unspeakable creatures of the
Nether have senses way beyond our own and may sense (or even see
you) in the blanket of fog which coats the dark dimension. For this
reason it is also advisable to use the buildings as cover as much as
you can. Make sure though that you don't end up in a situation where
you can potentially become trapped in a confined space without any
way of getting out. You must always make sure you have an escape
route. Tactical and sensible retreats are a vital tool when battling a
Nether related incident. If you simply rush into danger you are not
going to survive for very long at all.

It is advisable not to have a strong scent if you are going to venture
into the Nether or go on a mission that may involve creatures and

entities of the Upside Down. Do not use strong perfumes or soaps, aftershave lotion, or deodorant. It may be wise to muddy your clothes with Nether 'dust' from the ground to negate any residual fragrance your clothes might have from washing powder. Make sure though that you have your face covering on and don't get this dust in your mouth or up your nose. Breath through your nose and out of your mouth in the Nether. This will stop you from getting tired too quickly and prevent your mouth from drying out too much.

Do not stop in one place for too long in the mirror dimension unless you are absolutely sure that this place is temporarily safe. You must remember that nowhere in the Nether is entirely safe for very long. Danger potentially lurks around each and every corner and can strike at any time. If one is in the Nether with someone else or even as part of a group you should obviously stay close together and not get separated. Numbers will give you greater strength and firepower in any encounter and you can also help one another if someone should become sick or get injured. Be careful though not to communicate too loudly. Lower your voices and try not to constantly talk.

It would make sense for you to tie a connective rope (rather as mountain climbers do) between any colleagues in the Nether so that no one can get separated and lost. Make sure you have the means to quickly dispense with this rope though if the situation calls for it. Though it may sound harsh and cold, you would not want to become bound to someone who is dead or fatally injured. In such a situation you must seek to preserve your own life. If your colleague is not fatally injured and will most likely survive then you should of course go to their aid and stay bound to them. They shall need your assistance to survive. If the situation were reversed you would need their assistance too.

There is contradictory evidence regarding the weather conditions in the Nether. There have been reports of strong winds but other reports indicate that the dimension is serene and deathly quiet. One should be prepared for the possibility of electrical storms and should this happen you are advised to seek shelter until the worst has passed. Remember what we have said about shelter in the Upside Down though. Do not on any account take refuge in a position where you might potentially become trapped. Given the parallel nature of the mirror dimension you should though be able to find plenty of familiar buildings or houses which can be used as a relatively safe (if temporary) refuge.

You must above all be aware that the longer you remain in the Nether the more precarious your situation will become. Inside the Nether you are essentially residing in a toxic atmosphere and shall be prey to all manner of lethal creatures. You must seek to escape as quickly as possible. All the documented evidence dictates that a rift back to our dimension should exist somewhere and it shall be up to you to find this portal back to the safety of our own reality. Do not cease searching for the portal because it will truly be the difference between life and death. Though your situation may seem bleak at times take heart from the fact that others have ventured into the Nether and lived to tell the tale. Survival in the mirror dimension is not at all easy but it is not impossible either.

* The first sensory deprivation tank (or chamber) was invented by John C. Lilly in 1954. Lily was an American physician, neuroscientist, psychoanalyst, psychonaut, philosopher, writer and inventor. The idea of sensory deprivation tanks is that you are removed from all external stimuli as a means to explore the nature of human consciousness. Test subject 011 is believed to have gained her powers of telekenisis from her mother's participation in MkUltra in the 1960s. Project MKUltra was a top secret CIA funded experiment into mind control that made use of the mind-altering drug LSD. MKUltra was a response to fears that the Soviets were more advanced in brainwashing and mind control techniques. The MKUltra experiments included remote viewing and extrasensory perception. Electroshock therapy was also used.

There is evidence that the CIA 'branched' out some of the MKUltra experiments to other nations like Canada and Sweden. Some of the participants in the experiments had no idea they were part of a government project. This was obviously highly unethical - hence the great secrecy. Project MKUltra ended in 1973 and only became public knowledge after the experiment was terminated. Believe it or not, it was a filing error which made the project come to light. They failed to destroy all the documents related to the experiments. Future administrations in the White House had to condemn the project and promise not to do anything similar. Most of the MKUltra experiments took place between 1953 and 1964. It has been speculated that Ted Kaczynski, better known as the Unabomber, was experimented on as part of MKUltra when he participated in a series of experiments at Harvard.

** An obvious concern for the government authorities in Indiana was making sure that foreign rivals did not learn about the existence of the Nether. There was a fear that rival nations might seek to somehow exploit the Nether and try to use it as a biological weapon (though how they might have done such a thing is rather vague) because this could be profoundly dangerous. These fears were later proven to perfectly valid because we have evidence that the Soviet Union learned of the existence of the Nether and attempted to make contact with the parallel world. The Soviets were hamstrung though by their lack of knowledge concerning the mirror dimension. Their attempts to access the dimension usually met with deadly failure and loss of life.

UPSIDE DOWN

I need hardly remind the reader that the Upside Down Nether conforms to what we could describe as the Lovecraftian ethos. There is still much that we don't know when it comes to this field of dark science and perhaps much that we can never hope to completely understand. The limited amount of knowledge available merely reminds us that the mirror dimension is exceptionally dangerous and must be approached with extreme caution and care. This is not a place that one can idly venture into with no preparation. You must expect the unexpected and always be prepared. You'll need the right equipment and you must make sure you do your research. Hopefully, this document will be of some assistance in preparing you for the trials and challenges that Nether related trouble will surely pose.

An eminent professor (who must remain nameless) was once secretly employed by a covert branch of the United States government to establish how the young boy in Indiana was able to miraculously survive for so long in the Upside Down. This was a valid and fascinating question because, as we have noted, many others who have ventured into this mysterious void have perished in short order and found the Nether an impossible place to survive. The boy who outlasted all others in the mirror dimension had no survival equipment nor any military or scientific training. He had no weapons save for an air rifle - a weapon which is hardly likely to make much of a dent on the super tough skin of a Demogorgon. So how was he able to survive in a place where trained scientists and heavily armed soldiers had died so easily and so swiftly?

The boy is believed to have been trapped in the Upside Down for several days before he was rescued. The scientists at the lab knew that the child was trapped in the Nether but they - as far as one can tell - assumed that he must be dead. It apparently never occurred to them that he might have survived because they considered such an eventuality to be impossible. Even if they had suspected he was still alive it is open to question whether or not they would have actually tried to rescue him. That sounds cold and callous for good reason. It WAS cold and callous.

The scientists in question were disgraced by this whole affair and replaced. The chief scientist at the lab eventually allowed a police officer and the boy's mother to enter the Nether and rescue the child. This was only done though in return for information regarding the location of test subject 011. The case files regarding this incident are sketchy and vague - not to mention missing many pages. For understandable (if hardly admirable) reasons, the scientists at the lab were in no mood to ever discuss the case of the child they left stranded in the Nether.

At best they seemed indifferent to the fate of this child. No concerted attempt was made to venture into the Nether to see if he was alive (no doubt the scientists would argue though that their attempts to explore the mirror dimension were frustrated by the deadly creatures who inhabited this decayed world). The main concern of the scientists was the recovery of test subject 011. The missing boy was - shamefully - rather forgotten as a consequence. The actions of the scientists in this case were both unprofessional and cold-hearted. They should have made a more committed and thorough effort to establish if the boy could be saved. It is evident that this was never done.

An obvious conclusion to draw from the incident involving the boy is that it IS possible to go into the Nether, somehow survive, and get out safely or, as in this case, be rescued. The police officer and the boy's mother did have an advantage though in that they had access to the main portal rift at the laboratory. They were able to use the rift to get out again once they had found the child. If you find yourself in the Nether unexpectedly then you probably won't enjoy any such advantage because, in most cases, you won't automatically know where the exit might be. As we have noted though, you should be encouraged by the fact that there SHOULD be an exit somewhere and it may, with any luck, be closer than you think.

The conclusion of the professor concerning the miracle of the boy who survived in the Nether for a week was hardly academic or complex but it was perfectly logical and revealing in its simplicity. He concluded that the child most likely survived for so long because he was simply very good at hiding. Sometimes the simplest explanations are the ones which make the most sense and that certainly pertains to the mystery of how the boy was able to survive in a place where no one else had lasted for very long at all. Though his ordeal was difficult and unpleasant he did manage to survive.

The lab in Indiana had sent scientists on cables into the Nether before and retracted the cable to find nothing left of the poor unfortunate scientist in question - save for a few splats of blood and tissue. After grim experiences like this you can perhaps understand why they allegedly gave little thought to the possibility that the boy might still be alive in the Upside Down. Not that this absolves the lab regarding their conduct. There is no way they could have known for certain if the child was really dead (though, as we have noted, it is understandable if they felt it likely he hadn't survived) and should have made a more concerted effort to establish his fate.

The most shocking thing about this case is that the chief scientist at the lab seemed strangely indifferent to the fate of the lost child. He seemed much more concerned with the retrieval of test subject 011. The boy was apparently able to take refuge in the Upside Down version of his family home and use his knowledge of the local geography of the town and surrounding area to his advantage. It is important to note at this juncture that a significant difference between the child and most of the soldiers and scientists who ventured into the Upside Down is that that the government agents sought either confrontation in the Nether or were looking for signs of life.

In other words, the soldiers and scientists were essentially on a collusion course with danger. The boy was merely content to stay out of sight - which would partly explain why he had more success in surviving. One can take heart from the unexpected survival of the child in the hazardous mirror dimension for so long. It proves that survival in the Nether is not impossible - though it certainly isn't easy or something you would wish upon yourself or anyone else.

It is believed that the boy did undertake some limited exploration of the Upside Down while he was trapped there but he confined most of his time in the mirror dimension to the family home and his woodland clubhouse. His movements were increasingly constricted by the heavy toll that the atmosphere of the mirror dimension extracted from him. He became increasingly fatigued and weary the longer he was trapped in the mirror dimension. This appears to be an unavoidable by product of the Nether so you must assuredly do as much as you can in the way of searching for an exit while you still have good reserves of energy and health.

The lab file on the boy indicates that he would not have survived for much longer if he hadn't been found. His repository system had suffered dreadfully and exhaustion had made all movement a struggle. He was bereft of energy and finding it more and more difficult to breathe. This indicates that while survival in the Nether is possible it is not possible for very long. You will have a limited window of opportunity where your energy and health is sufficient to search for a portal and - if need be - fight for your survival against predators. Make valuable use of this time. You must seek to escape from the Nether while you still have the fighting strength to do so.

The boy was apparently able to somehow manipulate electricity in our reality from the confines of the Nether in order to communicate with his mother in our dimension. Though complex and vague, this does indicate that a form of communication between the two realities

is not impossible. It is therefore advisable to have a knowledge of
MORSE CODE. According to Wikipedia - 'Morse code is a method
of transmitting text information as a series of on-off tones, lights, or
clicks that can be directly understood by a skilled listener or
observer without special equipment. It is named for Samuel FB
Morse, an inventor of the telegraph. Each Morse code symbol
represents either a text character (letter or numeral) or a prosign and
is represented by a unique sequence of dots and dashes. The dot
duration is the basic unit of time measurement in code transmission.

'The duration of a dash is three times the duration of a dot. Each dot
or dash is followed by a short silence, equal to the dot duration. The
letters of a word are separated by a space equal to three dots (one
dash), and the words are separated by a space equal to seven dots. To
increase the speed of the communication, the code was designed so
that the length of each character in Morse is approximately inverse
to its frequency of occurrence in English. Thus the most common
letter in English, the letter "E", has the shortest code, a single dot.
Morse code is used by some amateur radio operators, although
knowledge of and proficiency with it is no longer required for
licensing in most countries.

'Pilots and air traffic controllers usually need only a cursory
understanding. Aeronautical navigational aids, such as VORs and
NDBs, constantly identify in Morse code. Compared to voice, Morse
code is less sensitive to poor signal conditions, yet still
comprehensible to humans without a decoding device. Morse is,
therefore, a useful alternative to synthesized speech for sending
automated data to skilled listeners on voice channels. Many amateur
radio repeaters, for example, identify with Morse, even though they
are used for voice communications. In an emergency, Morse code
can be sent by improvised methods that can be easily "keyed" on and
off, making it one of the simplest and most versatile methods of
telecommunication.'

If someone you know is trapped in the Nether it might be worthwhile
putting out electrical lights which conform to an alphabet. If the
person on the other side is inventive and determined enough they
should be able to harness these lights to send you a message. This
form of communication is essentially akin to an electrical Ouija

Board. The relationship between energy and the two dimensions is something that we don't yet understand but it is nonetheless encouraging that some form of communication through electrical manipulation appears to be possible between the two realms.

You are - should you find yourself trapped in the Nether - encouraged to explore this form of electrical communication should you consider your situation to be desperate. It may be a way to send for a search party to come and find you in the Nether. It is also a means for you to indicate that you are still alive in the mirror dimension. If one runs a hand through the vicinity of light bulbs in the Nether you should detect a field of energy which will resemble glitter when touched. Your manipulation of this field of energy should have an effect on the parallel light bulbs in our reality.

The boy trapped in the Nether for a week was able to find a portal between the two worlds - although he was unable to breach the portal himself and get home. The portal he discovered was most likely a temporary portal created by the Demogorgon. This portal may have closed up before he was able to use it as a way to navigate home. The main portal rift was in the lab but it seems evident that the child failed to locate this particular portal (he was patently unaware that a portal resided in the lab). The lesson from this case is that you must try and get to portals before they start to close.

As portals close they apparently begin to develop a thick membrane which eventually becomes too tough for a human to break through. If you can get to one of these portals early though you should stand an excellent chance of forcing your way through. If you do become trapped in the Nether and find one of these portals you should do everything you can to break through. The trapped boy was hampered by the fact that he ended up in the Nether suddenly and unexpectedly. As a consequence of this he had no equipment or tools - like a knife or axe - which might have helped break through the tough portal skin. You should make sure that you are much better prepared in the way of supplies - even if you aren't planning a trip to the Nether. There is always a chance that you might end up there unexpectedly like the child in question.

If one should become trapped in the Upside Down it is advisable to be constantly alert lest a portal should reveal itself. One can never be sure were and when they might appear. Demogorgons seem to have the ability to open little dimensional rips in order to move back and forth between realities. Though risky and dangerous, it is therefore important to notice any Demogorgon activity or movement in the Nether because this may supply you with an escape door back to our world. If a Demogorgon is sighted then that could mean that a portal is somewhere in the immediate vicinity.

One should stress though that exposure to a Demogorgon will be fatal in most circumstances. You must ideally access the portal (should one appear) without engaging the Demogorrgon or attracting its attention. Such a task will not be easy and you must muster all the cunning and stealth you can to achieve this. There have been no reported instances of Demogorgons using portals as traps to bait human prey but such an eventuality can not be completely ruled out. Demogorgons do have a degree of cunning and one must never underestimate this. Only try to access a temporary portal if you think it is safe. There is obviously no point in racing towards a portal rift if you are simply going to run straight into a lurking Demogorgon. You are highly unlikely to survive in this rather unwelcome scenario.

In order to stop the Nether from encroaching into our reality, scientists in the United States have found that flamethrowers are a reasonably effective (if time consuming and dangerous) means of doing this. Fire seems to be one weapon that reaps some rewards when deployed against the Upside Down and its native creatures. We will discuss some of the ways you might be able to use fire against Nether threats later in the book. The fact that fire was able to temporarily contain the Nether from spreading into our dimension from the depths of a lab was an encouraging development because it did indicate that the shadow world had a weakness and was not invincible.

Our ability to access the Upside Down is believed to have arose unwittingly. We know from intelligence agency reports that the Soviet Union learned of the existence of the Nether in the early 1980s but their attempts to gain access through a specially constructed drilling machine were unsuccessful. Not much is known about this machine because it was largely destroyed in 1985 and

secret Soviet military scientific documents from that era are
impossible to obtain - should they even exist anymore. The machine
looked rather like a large jet engine according to first hand accounts.
A portal rift is the only known safe way to get in or out of the Upside
Down and such machines as the Soviets constructed to breach the
mirror dimension were unreliable to say the least.

Many mistakes, as George Sarton might say, were made by the
scientists in both the United States and the Soviet Union in their
investigations of the Nether. You might say that their curiosity and
haste to chart this new dimension needlessly cost lives. It is believed
the Soviet attempts to access the Upside Down were a result of
pressure from the military establishment and the political masters in
Moscow. They gave little thought to the impossible task they were
placing scientists under and didn't seem to care if lives were lost
attempting to manipulate a way to cross dimensions. Sadly, it
appears that scientists and soldiers were deemed expendable in the
top secret Soviet mission to access the mirror dimension.

As for what the Soviets actually wanted with the Nether I'm afraid
we can only speculate. One might posit the theory that the mirror
dimension was rather akin to the space race or the Cold War nuclear
arms race. The Soviet sense of themselves as a great power was
bound up in their 'competition' with the United States and the West.
The Soviets were clearly uncomfortable at the knowledge that the
Americans had opened a rift to a hitherto unknown dimension (we
must assume that Soviet spies in the United States had deduced that
a rift had been opened in Indiana and sent this news back to
Moscow) and so desired to do the same thing. They feared that the
discovery of the mirror dimension might hand the United States
some sort of strategic advantage. Perhaps the Soviets were fearful
that the Nether might be harnessed as a new biological weapon
which could render their own conventional military forces obsolete.

The Soviet motivation to breach the mirror world might also have
had an economic motivation. At this stage in history the Soviet–
Afghan war had been waging for several years and the Soviets were
struggling to meet the economic cost of such a long and gruelling
conflict. The Soviet Union was economically weak in 1985 and only
had five years left before it dissolved and Moscow had to pull its

military forces out of Eastern Europe - which it had controlled since the end of the Second World War. Senior figures in the Soviet military and government establishment were well aware that the power of the Soviet Union was waning and that very difficult and testing times lay ahead. They knew that the Cold War was nearly over and that the United States and the West would be the victors.

The Soviets might have speculated that the Nether could yield valuable mineral resources or precious metals. Perhaps it might contain oil or gold. Maybe it might even contain a new source of energy that would change the world and make the nation who controlled this energy the richest country on Earth. These were all possible speculative considerations in the Soviet motivation to explore the mirror dimension. It was one last push for glory before the empire fell apart. An attempt to snatch victory from impending defeat. Whatever lay behind their great interest in the mirror dimension, one thing is certain. The Soviets were absolutely determined to view its mysterious secrets for themselves - whatever the human cost.

I should note at this juncture that there is - as of yet - no evidence the Nether contains any minerals or rare materials. It should be noted though that human exploration of the Nether has been extremely limited. We have barely scratched the surface when it comes to exploration of the mirror dimension. Just as the deep oceans of Earth retain many secrets and things we can't see or understand the same is doubly true of the mirror world. Empirical scientific and geological data is scant.

Given that the Nether is a parallel of our own world it doesn't seem outrageous to propose that it might possibly contain oil or valuable materials but we simply don't know for sure. An exploration of this realm purely for economic profit though would appear to be not only foolhardy but also strangely unethical. Any serious attempt to explore the Nether must be primarily scientific with the primary aim of making our dimension safer. Can you imagine a scenario where oil companies were drilling in the Nether? Such an insane and surreal state of affairs should never come to pass and with any luck it never will. Sadly though, one would not put it past certain nations to attempt this should they have the means to access the Nether.

The Upside Down conforms to some of the rules of our reality in that it has gravity and light - though that light is rather gloomy and hampered by dust and mist. It is also a mirror dimension in the true sense. If, for example, you find yourself in the Upside Down version of your own town then all the landmarks (library, shops, roads etc) should be present - only decayed and derelict. The Upside Down is essentially a ruined nightmare version of our own world bereft of human life and full of danger and strange creatures. It is an alienating and lonely experience to be trapped in the Nether and you must be prepared for the extreme sense of isolation you will face.

Some of the creatures of the Nether have been confirmed and encountered but it would seem logical to presume that the mirror dimension contains creatures that human beings have yet to encounter. Only a limited number of people (be they scientists or civilians) have entered the Nether or had dealings with the creatures of the mirror world so our knowledge concerning the full extent of its sentient life remains limited. This means that you must be on high alert for hitherto unclassified threats within (and of course outside) the Nether. Your dealings with any new creature should be circumspect and tentative because we know absolutely nothing of their abilities and strengths and weaknesses. An enemy that you know nothing about can be the most dangerous enemy of all. Do not engage any new unclassified creatures in the Nether unless you feel you have no option.

If you find yourself trapped in the Nether then you should be able to adopt at least some of the tactics that the boy in Indiana did in managing to survive. Look for familiar landmarks in the Upside Down. A house or building (like a school for example or even a house that you might have lived in) that you know well. Your knowledge of these properties should give you an advantage over the Demogorgons. You should know the best places to hide and the quickest way to get in and out without being detected.

It would make pragmatic sense to establish a place like this as a base or refuge in case of danger. A place where you know you can retreat to until the coast is clear. If at all possible establish more than one building to use in this fashion because you may have to abandon a refuge due to detection by Nether creatures. If you switch up your base of operations it will be more difficult for mirror dimension predators to know where you are at any given time. Familiar geography should be your friend inside the Nether. It should be at least a modicum of comfort to know that this barren realm will not be completely alien.

A retreat or refuge also gives one the option of ducking out of the wide open spaces and mist. You will be less vulnerable in such a place - though of course this is only a temporary measure in case of an emergency. We must repeat that your main priority must still be to find a portal and escape from the Nether as quickly as possible. It is unavoidable that you must go out in open spaces to look for a portal but such a course of action will of course be highly dangerous and make you more vulnerable. It cannot be stressed enough that you should always have your wits about you when you travel in the Nether. Stay as silent as possible and stay alert at all times.

According to all available evidence, it is not possible for sound to travel between the two dimensions unless one uses a portal. It may be possible to become audible across dimensions if you communicate next to a portal. The sound will distorted and not of a high volume. One can take encouragement from the fact that the portal rifts between dimensions appear to be thin and transmit at least SOME noise and also a degree of movement. It appears though that not all of them are breachable by force. This, as we have noted, could be a consequence of the fact that some of them have started to 'heal' and close up. This makes it imperative that you find any such portal as soon as possible before it begins to close and become too strong to get through.

The term Upside Down was coined unwittingly by test subject 011 when she used a Dungeons & Dragons board to illustrate to the missing boy's friends that he was trapped on the underside of our own reality. The children therefore came to speak of the dark dimension as The Upside Down or Vale of Shadows. This is clearly a reference to the Plane of Shadows. * The children evidently used Dungeons & Dragons (of which they were presumably avid players in the internet free age of the 1980s) as a sort of code or shorthand to make sense of the scientific concepts relating to the mirror dimension.

Dungeons & Dragons is a fantasy tabletop role-playing game (RPG) originally designed by Gary Gygax and Dave Arneson, and first published in 1974. Over fifty million people around the world have played Dungeons & Dragons since it was invented. The game has suffered from various controversies in its history. An organisation called B.A.D.D. (Bothered About Dungeons & Dragons) tried to get the game banned because they alleged it was turning its enthusiasts into occult obsessed Satanists. The Harry Potter books had to put up with similar nonsense when they became popular in later decades. The campaign seemed especially odd because Gary Gygax, the co-creator of the game, was a regular at church and as far away from a Satanist as you could get. Though it had a modest development budget, Dungeons & Dragons was soon incredibly popular. The fan base of the game today is surprisingly young with many enthusiasts under the age of 25.

Activity in the Nether can affect the electromagnetic field of the human world. It has been noted that the arrival of the Demogorgon (a creature we shall discuss in the next chapter) in our reality is often marked with electricity fluctuations and lights going on and off. This is obviously an important feature to notice because it will give you an early indication of potential danger. Think of it as an early warning system. It is not known how the creature generates enough energy to open portals and affect the electrical systems of our reality. Our understanding of these Nether creatures remains frustratingly incomplete.

The fact that the Demogorgon can apparently create portals makes it a more dangerous foe but, as we have noted, one compensation of this curious ability is that it might potentially given you a quick passage back to our reality should you become trapped in the Upside Down. One prevailing scientific theory is that the Nether was once a fairly ordinary alternate version of our own world - until it was taken over by the Shadow Monster aka the Flayer (an entity we shall also discuss later). If true this would provide an explanation for why the mirror dimension is now ruined and hostile - despite containing the familiar bric a brac of our own world.

This theory (if true) would indicate that the mirror dimension was ravaged by the Flayer. Perhaps there were even alternate human versions of ourselves in the mirror world who were made extinct by the Flayer's rampage. We simply can't say for sure as the Nether is not a place that readily gives up its secrets. The worrying thing about this theory is that it suggests that such a destructive fate is what the Flayer has planed for our dimension. As for the veracity of this theory, it remains open to speculation.

There have been no firm reports of human bones or remains found in the Nether (besides those of a doomed teenager named Miss Holland) but our exploration of this dark world has not been extensive enough to conduct a thorough search on this front. As a consequence of this the true nature and history of the Nether remains vague. A scientific dig in the Nether would be fascinating and potentially revealing but it is of course very unlikely that the creatures of the Nether would peacefully accommodate this and so such a project would be a near impossibility.

The Nether

It is not advised to use a flashlight too often in the Nether as the glare of the beam may attract unwelcome visitors to your vicinity. There will be occasions though where a flashlight will be valuable in the Upside Down. It may, for example, be helpful in allowing you to scan the floor for obstacles or be of vital assistance in assessing a wound or injury. You must be sensible though in your use of a flashlight in the mirror dimension. Only use it if you feel it is completely necessary.

The Nether appears to contain no familiar plant life also native to our own Earth and has its own unique ecosystem. This is made up of vines and membranes. It seems reasonable to propose that if the Mind Flayer is possibly a creature that has ravaged other dimensions it changes the ecosystem of each new dimension it vanquishes. The decayed flora of the Nether, as we shall see, seems to operate under a Hive Mind operated by the Flayer. This gives the Nether a degree of societal organisation and makes it more formidable. One shouldn't make the mistake of assuming the mirror dimension is a random place made up of dangerous individual creatures who act alone. The real truth appears to be far more complex and dangerous than that assumption.

The Nether is exceptionally dangerous and toxic and can pose a considerable hazard and obstacle as you attempt to move around in the mirror dimension. Take note - as much as you can without becoming distracted - of where your feet are going. The Upside Down has been known to create a tunnel system which then spreads underneath our own world. In the confines of these tunnels the toxicity of the Upside Down also seems to apply so one must make sure that face coverings are in place if you end up in one of these tunnels. These tunnels are slightly easier to escape from than the actual Upside Down because they are not, as far as we can tell, literally in ANOTHER dimension.

Not to say that escape from a 'nether' tunnel is a picnic though. The danger these tunnels pose should never be underestimated. Should you become trapped in one of these tunnels your circumstances could be every bit as precarious and dangerous as if you were actually trapped inside the Nether itself. One sign that you might be near one of these underground tunnels is that they tend to have a toxic effect on crops and plants that are growing above them. Case studies indicate that Upside Down tunnels also rot any nearby trees on the surface.

In the event of Nether related activity around your town be aware of these tell tale signs of rotted crops on farm land or open ground.

Even if you note that plants and trees in a suburban garden are looking very unhealthy this could be a byproduct of an Upside Down tunnel. It would be very foolhardy to go into an Upside Down tunnel alone and even more foolhardy to do so without telling anyone where you have gone. If you venture into one of these tunnels you will need back-up in case anything happens to you. You should make sure that someone is at hand and pull you back up to safety. They might even have to come in and rescue you should the deadly flora of the tunnels have an adverse effect.

The tunnels can be very deep in places so please make sure you have a rope or ladder in place somewhere which would enable you to climb back up to the surface. You may well encounter Nether creatures in one of these tunnels so please be aware that they are potentially as highly dangerous as the Nether itself. Given the fact that the Upside Down and its tunnels tend to be clogged with tendrils and vines it is very advisable to make sure that you always have a knife of excellent cutting quality among your provisions.

A compass may be of some use during a Nether crisis but be aware that the strange electromagnetic interference caused by the Upside Down and portals can often make compass readings unreliable. A compass may be of significant use in the Nether because it may possibly be affected by the energy created by a gate and thus lead you to one. We know that portals in our reality affect compass readings (which should enable you to find a portal in our dimension should the situation require you to do so) but though the science on the reverse situation is not entirely proven it would appear to be something worth exploring should one become trapped in the mirror world.

Your greatest asset in the Upside Down, if survival is to be at all plausible, will remain your wits and ability to stay calm even in the most extreme circumstances. You must maintain your focus and concentrate on constructive efforts to escape from your predicament with the minimum of risk. Though water is scarce in the Upside Down it is advisable to keep your survival kit in a waterproof bag due to the damp and fetid environment of the Nether.

There has been a case study where the creepers and vines of an

Upside Down tunnel went to great lengths to avoid running water. This is an important detail to remember and indicates that the Nether and its associate life does not like water very much. As we shall see later though, this is once again a complex sphere of Nether related science for there has been evidence of a dimensional portal located at the bottom of a lake. We will discuss this apparent contradiction later in our document.

It is recommended that your Upside Down survival kit should contain some food. It is obviously not practical to carry too much food (especially if you aren't expecting to go into the Nether in the first place) but it might save your life if you DO unexpectedly end up in the mirror dimension. Perishables like fruit or bread are obviously not recommended but small longer lasting items like energy bars, nuts (which are easy to carry and will provide you with valuable energy and protein), dried fruit, and chocolate could be the difference between starvation and survival if you find yourself trapped in the Upside Down.

If you have something you can eat in the Nether it will preserve your strength and energy for longer and also help you concentrate. A starving person constantly thinking about food is simply going to be distracted by their hunger. A canteen of water is also of course essential. It is obviously not recommended that you attempt to eat anything you find in the Nether as it is likely to be highly toxic. Any rations you have should ideally be in a package and be the sort of food that doesn't give off an odour.

If one were to have a 'smelly' food in the Nether it would potentially give your presence away. Demogorgons are believed to have an excellent sense of smell and would certainly notice if you were brazenly (and stupidly) eating something that activated their olfactory system unnecessarily. Be very aware of this potential danger when you choose your provisions. Things like energy bars should be fairly neutral in terms of smell and should be safe to carry and eat.

One item that might be useful to have upon your person in the Nether are boiled sweets. These will stop your mouth from becoming too dry and keep thirst at bay (thus preserving your water supply for longer). Having a boiled sweet will also help you maintain your focus. Do not use menthol sweets though because these definitely will dry your mouth out. You should ration your provisions as much as possible. Humans can survive for three days without water and much longer without food but you will need some sustenance and liquid in the end if you become trapped in the Nether. Your primary goal is to escape from the Nether before lack of water and food becomes a serious problem.

It would be sensible to control your breathing in the Nether and not become anxious if at all possible. Keep yourself occupied with a clear plan of action - which in this case is obviously going to be escaping from the Nether as quickly as possible. You must maintain a positive outlook no matter how bleak the situation might appear to be. A positive mental attitude is vitally important in difficult situations. One should also conserve energy as much as possible. Try not to wear yourself out too quickly.

It is not recommended to carry any alcohol in an Upside Down crisis. While alcohol might be useful for cleaning a wound you'd be better off with antiseptic cream. Alcohol will simply dehydrate you and cloud your senses if you drink it. If you encounter any creatures native to the Upside Down your first instinct might be to run but in some circumstances this could be counter productive and activate the creature's hunting instinct. You may simply be drawing attention to yourself if you take obvious flight.

There are going to be situations in the Nether where you have no choice but to break cover and run but if at all possible you should stay hidden and silent. The Nether is the worst place to battle a Demogorgon because these creatures are on their own territory. They will be much more at home than you in the mirror dimension and biology has doubtless adapted them to the toxic atmosphere and poor visibility. Though it might be difficult your main strategy in the Nether should be to avoid the creatures of this mirror dimension altogether.

It is important to keep warm in the Upside Down and one important tip is make sure that you have a hat of some some sort - preferably a warm woolly one. We lose body heat from the top of our head so a hat is an important survival item in the cold and chilly confines of the Nether. An important (if strange) survival tip is that you'll stay warmer if you empty your bladder. One must of course though only do this in a spot you deem relatively safe (safe places are admittedly rather difficult to find in the Nether).

If you are bitten by something in the Nether construct a ligature to control where the blood does (or indeed doesn't) flow. It is important that you wash the wound with clean water and cover it with a plaster or bandage. Plasters and bandages should be an essential part of your supplies for any Nether expedition. There have been instances where sentient slug like creatures of the Nether have embedded themselves into the flesh of a human being. This Nether parasite matter will cause an infection which will spread. There is evidence that these pieces of Nether matter have the ability to take over human hosts. One should therefore be very careful to avoid such a fate by not getting bitten in the first place.

If you do end up with an Upside Down slug embedded in your flesh you must remove it as quickly as possible. This will be easier said than done and most likely very painful but the consequences of not doing anything are probably going to be a lot worse. If you can remove the piece of Nether parasite matter then it should - so long as you have acted with haste - mean that it is no longer possible for the creature to take control of your body and mind.

As for the lingering effects of a brief Upside Down infection of this nature we know little but it seems safe to say that there will be some discomfort and a possible mental connection to the Flayer. Anyone who has experienced something like should naturally be watched very closely by their friends and colleagues and undertake a medical check. We shall discuss matters relating to the Flayer in more depth in a later chapter.

Some civilians who have survived a trip to the Upside Down have reported that they experienced ground tremors and what felt like small earthquakes while they were in the mirror dimension. This would indicate that the Nether can be an unstable place. One should therefore be prepared for such an eventuality. If you do experience ground tremors and instability then you should make sure that you hold onto something (like a tree for instance) until the disturbance subsides. If one were to fall due to these tremors you may get injured. You must avoid such a fate.

The fantastical and outlandish theory that the Nether is actually a future version of our own reality has gained a surprising amount of traction in secret government circles over the years but one would be at a loss to explain why this should be the case. Most of those who have returned from the Nether report that the artifacts and objects of the mirror dimension (like cars, buildings, and street signs) conform roughly to the time in which these experiences took place. No one in the Nether has seen cars and buildings from a bygone age nor a futuristic one.

As far as we can tell, if you enter the Nether in the current year and then it will be the current year in both realities - though of course years and dates have little meaning in the mirror dimension. Now, having said this, there is evidence that a Nether entity has contradicted this theory and seems to have the ability to manipulate time - or our conception of time at the very least. We will discuss this matter more fully later in our document.

Attempts by a scientific lab to take readings in the mirror dimension might have provided more conclusive evidence in relation to this time contradiction theory but scientific exploration of the Upside Down was constricted by the atmospheric conditions and the dangerous creatures who reside there. The Nether is decidedly not a very suitable place for a scientific field trip. The creatures of the Nether are hardly likely to stand idly by as scientists conduct a field trip. It is believed that attempts by the lab in Indiana where the 1983 rift opened to gather data concerning the Nether were frustrated by fatalities involving scientists who entered the portal. One can hardly be surprised if the lab in question ran out of willing participants after these grisly deaths.

It should be noted that it is not always applicable to transfer conventional survival skills or tactics to the Upside Down. The two scenarios simply can't be compared because the Nether represents a completely unique and fantastical challenge. If one were attempting to survive a harsh environment in our reality there are basic sensible things to do - like build a fire for instance. Such a course of action would be pointless and dangerous in the Nether. Taking the time to build a shelter would also be pointless in the Nether because it is hardly a place where you can reside for any length of time. Your best bet is to find a building as a refuge but aside from using it as a last resort you should keep moving in the hope of finding an exit.

One might venture though that some tracking skills may be of use in the Nether as a means to gauge movement of other creatures and their relative proximity to oneself. Given the preponderance of ash and dust in the Nether it may be possible (with the use of a flashlight given the gloom and lack of light) to discern footprints on the Nether floor where the ground is even enough to allow for such a scenario. The Demorgorgon is a large creature with a considerable mass. It is logical to assume that such a beast will leave impressions on the surface of the Nether in some form - though the dust of this decayed realm may cover those tracks. You may be able to make use of these temporary indents to discern where the creature has been or might be heading.

Above all, be very careful not not to get too distracted in the Nether. Your main focus in the Nether should be to stay alert. Listen carefully for any sign of movement and stay sharp. Your very life will depend on how sharp your senses are. We must stress again that you must not panic in the Upside Down. It is understandable that you will be frightened and suffering from some anxiety but it is important that you try your best to stay calm and not make any stupid decisions. Remember that others have ventured into the mirror dimension and survived. You must have faith that you will be like them and eventually emerge safe and sound from the nightmare reality back into the safety of our own dimension.

* The Plane of Shadow is described by ForgottenRealms in the following way - 'The most striking and immediate impression a visitor to the Plane of Shadow experienced was the lack of color and light; no sun, moon, or stars adorned the vault of the inky black sky, and all things looked as if the color had leeched out, leaving nothing but black and white, which in the dimness were more like "dark black" and "light black". A light source only illuminated half the distance it normally would, flames and fires put out less heat, and

spells that dealt with light or fire were less predictable and prone to failure, whereas shadow spells were enhanced.

On the other hand, although it would not illuminate as far, any light source on the plane could be spotted at a distance of up to ten times its normal range of illumination, such was the contrast to the constant gloom, similar to a star in the night sky. Even a light source that only put out shadowy illumination, like a darkness spell or a lantern burning shadowlight oil, could be seen up to five times its range of illumination. The morphic nature of the Shadowfell could produce strange effects, mainly in areas like the Black Rift that were especially morphic, and with events that had a particular affinity with the plane, like death. For example, in the Black Rift alone, a pile of bodies caused more skeletons to appear, until there were thousands.

More bizarre were the strange biers upon which dead bodies spontaneously appeared, apparently drawn from wherever they rested, anywhere in existence, only to disappear after a few seconds, presumably to wherever they'd come from. Stalactites in a cave dripped ephemeral shadowstuff, which was reabsorbed into the plane rather than form a puddle. Even common mushrooms bore realistic humanoid faces, capable of twitching or blinking. More significantly, forests of grasping tendrils sprouted from some surfaces and reached for passersby, similar to the black tentacles spell.'

DEMOGORGON

The name of this Upside Down creature was coined by friends of the boy in Indiana who was trapped in the Nether. They enjoyed Dungeons & Dragons and so used the name of a monster in the game to describe the dimensional creature which plagued their town in 1983. The term "Demogorgon" first appeared in the 4th Century Latin poem Thebaid by Placidus. The poem described a demon who must not be named. The term Demogorgon is believed to derive from a mistranslation of an old Greek manuscript. The Demogorgon in Dungeons & Dragons has two heads (something which the Nether version of this creature patently does not share). The heads are named Aemeul and Hethradiah. The Demogorgon made its first Dungeons & Dragons appearance in the 1976 game Eldritch Wizardry.

Demogorgons are the most common creatures of the Nether. You might say they are the foot soldiers of the Upside Down. If there is an Upside Down infestation or breach in your town then the chances of encountering a Demogorgon are relatively high. In the event of dimensional trouble in your vicinity it should be expected that a roaming Demogorgon may be at large. There could even be more than one or Demogorgons at a different stage of their development.

You must learn as much as you can about these creatures before such an eventuality because they present a deadly and formidable challenge. The more you know about Demogorgons the better chance you will have of surviving an encounter with one - or, even better, avoiding an encounter altogether. Demogorgons are ruthless, cunning, and exceptionally powerful and brutal. They are exceptionally dangerous and not to be taken lightly.

Because the Demorgorgon is so large and looks so alien some eyewitnesses reported that they were frozen with fear when they first encountered the beast. While it is obviously going to be impossible not to experience some degree of fear and horror while facing a Demogorgon for the first time it is important that you try to control this fear and do not freeze. You must continue to act according to some of the tactics and strategies we will continue to set out in the rest of this volume.

The first thing you should be aware of is the fact the Demogorgons tend to lurk in the shadows but then strike without fear or mercy when an opportunity presents itself. This obviously makes them terrifying antagonists. You can though, with the right tactics and preparation, mitigate at least some of the threat posed by this fearsome and inexplicable monster. You will need to be brave though to employ these tactics. Any Nether related activity involving a Demogorgon is going to be a challenging and frightening affair. Take solace though from the fact that a number of civilians have encountered a Demogorgon and survived to tell their tale.

Demogorgons do not appear to have eyes but they do have
heightened senses and are natural hunters. We simply don't know
what sort of vision Demogorgons may or may not have but those
who have survived an encounter with the creature all testify that it
has no discernible facial features. The blank featureless head of the
creature adds to the foreboding and indifferent aura of doom it
radiates. One scientist had a theory that proximity to the
Demogorgon causes bleeding from the ears and nose in humans but
this has never been verified and has no evidence to support the
theory. One may therefore be confident is stating that the theory is
flawed and simply an urban myth (in so far as urban myths can
flourish in secret scientific and military circles).

It is believed that, given their apparent lack of eyes, Demogorgons
may hunt primarily by means of sound and smell. Their senses
appear to be considerably more acute than those of human beings.
Some contend that Demogorgons can detect the minute and small
vibrations created by movement on the ground. If you are being
stalked by a Demogorgon you are advised to keep still (when
possible) and be as quiet as possible. You must use extreme stealth
to avoid detection. The arrival of a Demogorgon in the vicinity is
often marked by detectable growls and shrieks. Anyone with first
hand experience of a Demogorgon close encounter will learn to
distinguish these sounds from natural background noise and know
exactly what they mean.

Though shrewd and excellent at hunting, Demogorgons are not
invisible or completely silent. If you concentrate and stay sharp you
will have an excellent chance of knowing when one of these
creatures is nearby. You ability to do this will be the difference
between life and death. Demogorgons have freakishly long arms
(which obviously endow the creatures with a considerably longer
reach than human beings) and legs and are armed with powerful
claws. A rake from one of these claws would do grave and serious
damage to the fragile skin of a human. You must avoid close quarter
combat with a Demogorgon if at all possible because you will be
greatly disadvantaged and outgunned in such a battle.

One must avoid a direct confrontation with a Demogorgon where the
creature is at arm's length. Such a scenario would render any tactic

or strategy you might have to defeat the creature rather moot because you would be most unlikely to survive such a skirmish. You will need more subtle and varied tactics to defeat a Demogorgon. The mouth and the head of the Demogorgon somewhat resembles a Rafflesia arnoldi. Rafflesia arnoldii, the corpse flower or giant padma, is a species of flowering plant in the parasitic genus Rafflesia. The head of the Demogorgon opens up to resemble a starfish. Five fanged triangles will unfurl. It is important not to get too close to the creature lest this should happen as it will try and grip you with these pincers.

The unique nature of the Demogorgon's head make it an unmistakable creature. As we shall discuss shortly, the fanged multiple mouths of the Demogorgon become apparent at an early stage of its development. You should have no excuse for not identifying this creature - whatever stage in its development it may be in. The lead scientist at the Indiana lab allegedly concluded that Demogorgons were predictable and compared them to animal predators in our reality like big cats. This was certainly a simplistic observation - although not one completely bereft of truth. We have managed to build up a reasonable amount of information concerning the behaviour patterns of the Demogorgon so one could probably say they are not the most enigmatic of creatures.

It should be noted though that, despite his hubris, the scientist in question was unable to stop the Demogorgon - even with numerous heavily armed military government agents at his disposal. It was test subject 011 who finally halted the Demogorgon in Indiana. The fact that the scientist felt the Demogorgon was rather predictable in terms of its behaviour was of no consequence whatsoever in actually stopping the creature. The lesson of this is that the Demogorgon must not be underestimated. There is a lot more to defeating this creature than establishing a few casual observations about its behaviour patterns.

Demogorgons are believed to hunt mostly at night (though they have been sighted during the day) in our reality (it is doubtful that the concept of night and day exists in the Nether as it does in our dimension - the Upside Down is a world seemingly composed of permanent twilight gloom) and their natural instinct - like all animals

- is to seek cover and hide in the shadows. The Demogorgon who infiltrated our reality in Indiana in 1983 made considerable use of the local woodland and is believed to have killed at least two hunters in these woods while at large. The creature also killed a number of scientists and government agents and although its official kill count has never been released by the authorities one would suspect that it might have run into a dozen or so people at least.

In the event of an Upside Down incident in your town you must be very alert and careful when navigating areas like woodland because this precisely the sort of terrain where the Demogorgon will hide while it waits for a chance to strike. The boy who was trapped in the Nether reported that when he attempted to aim a rifle at the Demogorgon (in anticipation of it entering the family shed he was taking refuge in) the creature then suddenly - without warning - appeared behind him. This alarming evidence would certainly run contrary to the dismissive assertion of the chief scientist that the creature is wholly predictable. One would say that suddenly appearing behind a victim out of the blue is the complete opposite of predictable.

The Demogorgon is patently a creature with occasionally unfathomable abilities that should not be underestimated. It is believed that the portals the Demogorgon can open to travel between realities are only temporary. How the creature opens these dimensional rifts is unclear but suffice to say it takes a great deal of energy and power to do so.

The strength and durability of the creature is such that it can somehow survive these huge surges of energy. The dimensional rips created by the Demogorgon, as we have noted, eventually 'heal' and close over time.

One should bear this in mind if you are ever trapped in the Nether or wish to use a portal to look for someone. Time will not be on your side in such a scenario. You must move fast because there is no guarantee that the portal will be there for very long. This is why we have stressed that inside the Nether you should keep searching as much as possible and only rest when it is completely necessary. There will also be times when you need to stop and hide. Delays like this will be frustrating but they are unavoidable because it will be the difference between life and death.

According to all available evidence, Demogorgons can absorb tremendous amounts of damage and punishment and yet still function. They are incredibly durable and resilient. This is arguably their most formidable asset and the thing that, more than anything, makes them such difficult opponents. To put it mildly, Demogorgons are very, very tough. Those who have encountered Demogorgons say they are almost impossible to discourage with small arms fire. There is also evidence that Demogorgons have regenerative healing abilities and so are able to withstand and survive weapons bullets. Bullets evidently find it difficult to penetrate the tough skin of the creature and the healing factor would naturally take care of any wounds the beast did actually suffer.

Not to say that Demogorgons are completely impervious to damage but it would clearly take a considerable amount of firepower to put one down for the count. There is a 1983 case study of several government agents armed with machine guns who were unable to halt a Demogorgon in the constrictive location of a school corridor in Indiana. The confined space should, in theory, have given the agents an advantage and made it easier for them to shoot the creature at point blank range. Alas though, they were unsuccessful in their task and lost their lives as a consequence. Though the firepower of the agents was considerable (at that time their standard issue weapons were the Heckler & Koch MP5K submachine gun and the Beretta 92FS) it was insufficient to stop the creature. The Demogorgon shrugged off the bullets and simply kept coming forward. The speed at which the creature moved was also a hindrance to the agents.

With this in mind, it is logical to assume that a single person, even if they are armed with a gun, would have little chance of surviving a direct encounter with a Demogorgon in which they sought to engage the creature. The monster would not be halted by one gun - no matter how skilled that person was in using the weapon or how powerful that gun was. Besides, there is no guarantee you would even be able to hit the creature with any meaningful shot before it closed the distance and attacked you. It is recommended then that, if possible, one should avoid engaging a Demogorgon in direct combat if you are alone - even if you do have a firearm.

A gun may be useful as a means to (very briefly) distract the creature but it will not halt the Demogorgon. In such a scenario you should seek to take flight or hide rather than pointlessly attempt to fell the creature with bullets. If several military trained agents armed with machine guns couldn't stop the creature then you will patently be wasting your time directly taking on a Demogorgon alone with a solitary firearm. Even if you hit the creature with more than one shot its forward momentum is unlikely be affected by mere bullets. Be aware then that while guns may be useful at times in a Nether crisis they can also give one a false sense of security.

A more effective weapon than a gun when it comes to Demogorgons would be fire. Demogorgons, like all creatures, do not like fire. Fire can be an effective way to keep a Demogorgon at bay and there is eyewitness evidence of burn marks becoming visible on the creature's skin when subjected to fire. As we have noted, the scientists in Indiana used flamethrowers as a means to keep the spread of the Nether to a manageable degree. The biology of the Nether (and this obviously includes the creatures who reside there) likes it cold, murky, and damp. Fire is therefore an effective weapon to use against them.

Fire is unlikely to kill a Demogorgon but it will potentially make the creature stop or even retreat. All field reports concerning Demogorgons note that these are aggressive creatures who will attack on sight (and even sound and smell). One can not overstate how dangerous these creatures can be. If one is loose in your town then you must be exceptionally alert and careful. If you can set the creature on fire this will be considerably more effective than anything you might accomplish with a handgun.

When it comes to brute physical strength, Demogorgons are much bigger and stronger than human beings. In a one on one confrontation or fight with a Demogorgon a human being would be greatly outmatched and stand no chance whatsoever of survival. Demogorgons have a much longer reach than humans and can easily pick up and throw an adult sized human being. Even a strong and powerful adult male human would have no chance of fighting off a Demogorgon. It would be akin to a small child attempting to fight a grizzly bear - a completely futile encounter that could only end one way. Demogorgons are rarely - if ever - going to be defeated in a direct confrontation. To ward off or banish one of these creatures you will need strategy and stealth and preferably be part of a team. You must essentially outwit and outmanoeuvre creature if you are to stand any chance of defeating it.

While there is plenty of evidence that Demogorgons are crafty and quite intelligent it is not believed that they have the IQ of an average and reasonably intelligent human being. These are primarily creatures of instinct and as such one should be able to come up with a workable strategy to negate their obvious physical advantages. It is very advisable then not to engage a Demogorgon in combat - especially if one has no weapons. Such a course of action would be plain and simple suicide.

Even if one did have a weapon, one on one combat is still not advised. There is no firm evidence, for example, that a knife wound would be fatal to a Demogorgon and managing to engineer a scenario where plunging a knife into a Demogorgon would even be possible would be difficult and dangerous to say the least. Demogorgon skin is exceptionally tough and it would take considerable force to plunge a knife into the creature. Even if such a feat were somehow accomplished there is no guarantee that the Demogorgon would be appreciably affected by such an attack. If the creature is able to withstand machine gun fire from several soldiers it would seem logical to presume it could withstand the blade of a knife.

It is also advisable - if at all possible - not to bleed in the immediate vicinity of a Demogorgon due to their perceived ability to detect even the smallest traces of blood. It is believed that the demise of a teenager named Miss Holland by a swimming pool in Indiana was in part due to the fact that she sustained a cut hand that evening and sat out by the pool at night. When drops of blood from her wound fell into the water it attracted the Demogorgon. It should be noted though that the boy who was trapped in the Nether was not bleeding when he was hunted and captured by the Demogorgon. The creature is equally likely to strike even without the presence of any blood. The ability of the Demogorgon to detect blood has been likened to that of a shark. *

It is not insignificant to note that Miss Holland was out by the swimming pool all alone while the other teenagers present that tragic and harrowing evening were all in the house. This would support the generally held academic theory that Demogorgons will primarily (though not exclusively) look for isolated prey - which is a logical instinctive hunting tactic for any predator. This is an important detail to remember. If you are all alone in an Upside Down scenario then this is obviously going to make you more vulnerable. One should therefore be very aware of this fact and avoid such a scenario as much as you can.

The Demogorgon will see a lone and isolated individual as easy pickings. You must avoid this fate if at all possible. This will patently be more difficult if you are alone in the Nether (there might unavoidably be situations though where you are all alone in a dimensional crisis). In these situations stealth and caution are strongly advised. The Demogorgon appears to have the ability to somehow drag victims back to the dark mirror dimension where it resides. The creature is believed to exploit the opening of these portals between dimensions in order to hunt in our reality.

If one were to continue the shark analogy, you could say that our reality is the Demogorgon's version of shallow waters or the place where people swim. The creature was patently delighted to have discovered the rich hunting grounds afforded by our reality. If a Demogorgon is loose in your town then you can be sure that the main priority of the creature will be to hunt. No one in the immediate vicinity will ever be completely safe as long as the Demogorgon is at large. It is therefore important that you try to keep track of Demogorgon sightings and establish the general area that the creature resides.

It should be noted that the boy who was captured by the Demogorgon in our reality and then transplanted to the Nether was - unlike Miss Holland - able to escape from the clutches of the creature and survive in the mirror dimension. This is an encouraging detail to remember. Escape from the Demogorgon is possible. There has been a scientific theory that the boy was able to survive in the Nether because he wasn't actually there as long as we believe. He was missing for several days but one scientists suggested that time might not correlate in the Nether to our dimension and it could be the case that the child only spent hours or a few days in the Nether before rescue.

This theory proposes that to us it felt like the child was missing for a week but this wasn't actually the case. We have already noted though that there is questionable evidence for this theory. When he was spoken to by scientists in Indiana after his recluse, the boy gave no indication that he had only been in the Nether for a matter of hours. He had clearly been inside the mirror dimension for a number of days as far as he was concerned and his health certainly indicated this was indeed the case. There is still much we don't understand about the Nether and relationship between time in our world and the mirror dimension remains unclarified for the time being. There is no empirical data which proves either theory for certain.

The five stages of Demogorgon development are Pollywog, Frogogorgon, Catogorgon, DemoDog, and Demogorgon. A pollywog is a name for a tadpole and refers to the larval stage of both frogs and toads. The creature, at its earliest stage, will rather resemble a large slug and then then become vaguely frog-like. If one should encounter a 'baby' Demogorgon (Pollywog) under no circumstances, however endearing it might seem, should you attempt to domesticate the creature and keep it as a pet. The creature will inevitably soon grow much bigger and become highly dangerous. It will only be contained in a room or house for a short time. It is inevitable that the creature will escape in the end and this will occur sooner than you might think.

Treating these creatures in a sympathetic fashion might be human but it is exceptionally foolish. One must not allow sentiment to cloud logic. If you secretly shelter a Pollywog you will ultimately be placing your local community in future danger because you are essentially harbouring a young Demogorgon. The Pollywog will quickly go through the stages of Demogorgon development and almost certainly attract other Demogorgons (in whatever stages of development they may be in) to the vicinity. This is doubly the case with DemoDogs as they tend to hunt in packs. You should never on any account keep the existence of a Pollywog a secret. The relevant authorities MUST be informed and the creature must be placed in their custody. Placing the creature back in the Nether - if at all possible - is also advised as an option if you don't wish to come into contact with the authorities (it could be that you don't trust them or are wanted by them).

There is some evidence that a child in Indiana tried to keep a Pollywog as a pet in 1984 but ran into all manner of trouble when the creature rapidly grew and then escaped from the boy's bedroom. Under no circumstances should you make the same mistake as this child. The child in question is believed to have been harbouring under the delusion that the Pollywog was a rare species of frog. During the Frogogorgon stage of development the creature will sprout hind legs and develop sharp teeth. The Catogorgon stage (so named because the creature is about the same size as a cat) will see the creature develop the distinctive starfish type mouth of the Demogorgon.

There is no real excuse for not deducing that these creatures are from the Upside Down - no matter what stage of development they might be in. It should be very obvious that these creatures are not native to our own reality. If you have even the slightest doubt about the origin of a creature you find during a Nether crisis you should most certainly err on the side of caution. Do not allow scientific curiosity to fog logic. You must make note of the developmental stages of Demogorgon biology and make sure that you are able to identify any creature, however small, that might potentially have come from the Nether.

There is field evidence that young Demogorgons are a danger to animals (like cats and dogs) indigenous to our dimensional reality. When the Demogorgon is sufficiently grown it will also become a danger to humans. While the 'DemoDog' stage of the Demogorgon is smaller (as the name implies they have dog-like qualities though they are larger than dogs) they are still exceptionally dangerous. DemoDogs seem to share many of the qualities of full blown Demogorgons in that they have thick protective skin and an impressive degree of cunning and stealth. There is some field evidence that DemoDogs have more agility than full grown Demogorgons though this assertion is debatable as Demorgorgons have shown impressive agility despite their larger weight and size.

According to secret reports, DemoDogs have illustrated the ability to hunt as a pack and deploy team tactics. In 1984, a group of teenagers in Indiana were allegedly outflanked by DemoDogs at an old junkyard. This was an impressive display of stealth and cunning and illustrated how formidable the creatures can be - even prior to their full stage of development. The DemoDogs hunted as a team in this incident and their hunting instincts were advanced enough for them to use team tactics designed to outwit their intended prey - which in this case was a group of human teenagers. Given that DemoDogs, with their shorter stature and dog like dimensions and movement, are less conspicuous than full sized Demogorgons then one can readily see how dangerous a group of them hunting in a pack might potentially be.

It is believed that the teenagers had lured the DemoDogs to the junkyard with meat but were then surprised when a pack of the creatures turned up. They had evidently only expected a solitary DemoDog and assumed they would be able to trap a lone creature. The teenagers had presumably also underestimated how large the creature would be by now. You should avoid making similar mistakes. If DemoDogs are at large then there is a good chance they will be operating in a pack and even if the 'baby' Demogorgon was very small the last time you saw it you should not expect the creature to be the same size during your next encounter.

Evidence suggests that DemoDogs are slightly more vulnerable to small arms fire and bullets than full blown Demogorgons. At the very least they can rocked back by gunfire - which does at least give you a window of opportunity when it comes to escape. Eyewitness evidence is not exactly copious when it comes to DemoDogs but it would appear that they are more distracted by bullets than full blown Demogorgons. There has though been no firm empirical evidence which suggests that any part of DemoDogs is more vulnerable than others. The skin of the creatures is scaly and rock like. There is no obvious weak spot. Given the retractive nature of the heads of the creatures and lack of eyes this also affords little in the way of an obvious target.

The biology of the Demorgorgon seems to have adapted to make the creature not exactly invulnerable but certainly highly resistant to damage. Human beings, by comparison, are fragile creatures and easily injured. Demogorgon biology has clearly gone in a different direction - prompted no doubt by the hostile and harsh nature of the dimension from where they come. Demogorgons grow and develop at a rapid rate compared to humans. Demogorgon evolution and biology is concerned with making the creature independent and formidable as fast as possible. It is, to repeat ourselves, extremely inadvisable then to shelter a Pollywog even for a short period. Such a course of action is liable to land you in very big trouble. The creature you shelter will grow at a rapid rate and become a danger not only to you but to the wider community.

Despite their size and immense weight, Demogorgons are surprisingly quick. Their long legs enable them to cover the ground quickly and they can leap long distances. This makes it very unlikely that you could outrun one in open ground. Do not underestimate how fast Demogorgons can be. You might think you could easily run away from such a large and heavy creature but you'd probably be wrong about that. It is not a risk that is worth taking. A hiding place or shelter will be necessary to escape in such a situation.

Use natural cover like trees as much as you can if you deduce that a Demogorgon is lurking in some woodland you are moving through. It might be prudent to carry a flare for such a scenario. Anything that can distract the creature and buy you more time to escape will be invaluable. There is unverified evidence that Demogorgons have psionic powers. During his own encounter with a Demogorgon in 1983, the boy who was trapped in the Nether reported that the creature was able to unlock the interior of the shed he was hiding in from the outside. Evidence of Demogorgons using these powers are scant though aside from the Byers incident.

There appears to be plausible evidence that DemoDogs sometimes eat the flesh of their victims. A RadioShack employee was killed by DemoDogs in 1984 while attempting to restore the power at a

Department of Energy facility in Indiana during a dimensional crisis. According to eyewitness accounts, the DemoDogs were tearing at the flesh of the victim in the moments during and after his tragic demise. It certainly appeared to be the case that they were eating him after his death.

There is a theory that Demogorgons are sensitive to light due to the dark and gloomy nature of their natural habitat (which in this case is obviously the decayed mirror dimension). One government scientist suggested that Demogorgons might be discombobulated and dazzled and weakened by extra powerful flashlights or even spotlights. I'm afraid to say though that this is not a theory that ever gained much in the way of traction or attracted much academic support - and for good reason.

Given that Demogorgons don't even appear to have eyes it is rather difficult to see how they could be bamboozled and blinded by flashlights. There is no field evidence to support the hypothesis that Demogorgons (or indeed DemoDogs) are unable to function normally (that is to say hunt and stalk humans) in a well lit bright environment. There is credible eyewitness evidence that the Demororgon at large in Indiana in 1983 was sighted during the day. This would appear to thoroughly contradict any theory that Demogorgons are ultra sensitive when it comes to daylight.

If one is forced to confront a Demogorgon it would be sensible to deploy some animal traps to slow the creature down - though such devices can be difficult to obtain in certain jurisdictions. Please make sure though that you don't deploy any traps where any animal or indeed human might be. The safety of all life - both human and animal - in our own reality should never be forgotten during a Nether crisis. You should only deploy traps in a confined space (preferably an interior space) where you intend to lure the creature. Only use traps if you have completely eliminated any chance of it snaring anything other than a Demogorgon.

If one is in a situation where a pack of DemoDogs is at large it is advisable to retreat to a small and secure barricaded property which is constrictive enough to make it easier to defend. In such a situation it is advisable (if possible) to be part of an armed team. The doors and windows must be made secure. Such measures will not make it impossible for the creatures to gain entry but they will make it difficult. The ability to frustrate the Demogorgon in such fashion is always important because it will buy the intended prey (which will obviously be humans) more time to escape or prepare an attack.

The brute physical strength of the Demogorgon makes it unlikely that the house will remain secure indefinitely but you will now have time to set up a 'choke point' - in short the place where the Demogorgon is most likely to enter the house and will therefore sustain heavy damage in doing so because you will be waiting. It is very important to have an exit route up your sleeve in case of an emergency. Given the large dimensions of the Demogorgon it should be perfectly feasible to establish an exit which a human being can enter but a Demogorgon can not. A DemoDog will obviously be more complex on this front though and able to fit into smaller spaces than a Demogorgon.

Despite their shorter stature, one shouldn't underestimate the strength of DemoDogs. There have been cases where they have broken through polycarbonate windows and steel doors. Suffice to say, containing these creatures is very difficult and something which will only be a temporary measure. DemoDogs are also very good at digging tunnels. They will tunnel into a floor or wall if they believe this is their only means of escape. If you wish to lure a Demogorgon into a trap you may be able to do this with blood. Demogorgons, as we have noted, can detect blood across the two dimensions.

DemoDogs have been successfully herded into an area by means of a trail of meat but you should only do this if you have a fully prepared plan or believe you can guide the creature (or creatures) towards a rift which will send them back into the Nether. The last thing you want to do is attract a herd of DemoDogs with no plan of action. It is worth remembering at this point that DemoDogs present a unique challenge because they tend to run in a herd and hunt in packs. You must therefore be mobile if caught in open ground and watch your flanks carefully. DemoDogs have less brute strength than Demogorgons so it might be slightly easier to keep them at bay in a cabin siege situation. There is evidence that DemoDogs tend to go for windows so watch these carefully and make sure they are secure and barricaded.

It was estimated that in 1984, hundreds of DemoDogs managed to
infiltrate our reality during an incident in Indiana. They were
thankfully vanquished when the main portal was closed (thus cutting
off the Flayer's mental control of them) but the alarmingly high
number of these creatures in this specific dimensional crisis indicates
the gravity of the threat they pose. When you remember that this was
just one isolated incident in a small town which was rendered neutral
before it got out of hand (that is to say threatened the local civilian
population) then you can see how serious an even bigger crisis could
be. It stands to reason that the Flayer could potentially send
thousands of DemoDogs into our reality if it had access to our
dimension. This is why any Demogorgon related activity must be
dealt with as quickly as possible.

The inability of bullets to stop the Demogorgon has led to a theory
that the creature has no critical organs. This has not been verified (as
of yet no one has dissected a Demogorgon) but it would explain why
guns seem to have no fatal effect on the monster. One should again
be well aware that Demogorgons are implacable antagonists. They
can shrug off considerable damage and keep moving towards you.
One reasonably effective tactic is to keep a Demogorgon distracted
and off balance. A plucky teenager in 1983 allegedly had some
success in this regard when he used a nail spiked baseball bat on the
creature. This created enough time to deploy traps and fire against
the monster.

Demogorgon skin is exceptionally tough compared to human skin
and serves as a formidable protective barrier. There is also evidence
that Demogorgons have the ability to leap considerable distances - a
hangover perhaps from the DemoDog stage of their development. A
teenager named Miss Holland who was found deceased in the
Upside Down after an encounter with the Demogorgon was badly
decomposed when discovered but relatively intact. This indicated
that she hadn't been subject to grotesque violence or eaten. There is
consequently a theory that Miss Holland was cocooned after death to
be used as a food source or breeding chamber in this nightmarish
dimension.

The boy trapped in the mirror dimension was discovered in the Nether with some sort of tendril attached and elongated down to his throat. This would suggest that he was kept alive on purpose near the end. It could be that the survival of the child for so long in the Nether was a consequence of the fact that the tendril was feeding him nutrients and oxygen for a specific purpose. If this is the case then it seems plausible to believe that the boy would not have survived if left to his own devices.

At the time of writing the breeding habits of the Demogorgon remain vague and mysterious. The test subject known as 011 is reported to have seen a Demogorgon with an egg during one of her sensory deprivation 'jaunts' at the Department of Energy in 1983 but - frustratingly - she was never asked to elaborate on this. It is safe to assume that the numbers of Demogorgons run into many thousands in their own native dimension. A large outbreak of these creatures in our own reality would be a disaster. You must somehow prevent this happening at all costs.

* From American Museum & Natural History - 'Sharks are often portrayed as having an almost supernatural sense of smell. However, reports that sharks can smell a single drop of blood in a vast ocean are greatly exaggerated. While some sharks can detect blood at one part per million, that hardly qualifies as the entire ocean. Sharks do, however, have an acute sense of smell and a sensitive olfactory system--much more so than humans. Sharks' nostrils are located on the underside of the snout, and unlike human nostrils, are used solely for smelling and not for breathing. They are lined with specialized cells that comprise the olfactory epithelium. Water flows into the nostrils and dissolved chemicals come into contact with tissue, exciting receptors in the cells.

These signals are then transmitted to the brain and are interpreted as smells. Because of the extreme sensitivity of these cells, as well as the fact that the olfactory bulb of the brain is enlarged, sharks can detect minuscule amounts of certain chemicals. This varies, of course, among different species of sharks and the chemical in question. The lemon shark can detect tuna oil at one part per 25 million - that's equivalent to about 10 drops in an average-sized home swimming pool. Other types of sharks can detect their prey at one part per 10 billion; that's one drop in an Olympic-sized swimming pool! Some sharks can detect these low concentrations of chemicals at prodigious distances - up to several hundred meters (the length of several football fields)—depending on a number of factors, particularly the speed and direction of the water current.'

FLAYER

In Dungeons & Dragons, a 'mind flayer' is known as an illithid. 'An illithid, also called a mind flayer, was an evil and sadistic being, humanoid in appearance, but with a four-tentacled octopus-like head. These beings were feared throughout the Underdark for their telepathic abilities and usually were not without two or more slaves, mentally bound to each individual mind flayer. Although they cooperated to achieve a goal, they would back away at the first sign that something was not profitable to themselves. They were capable of speaking Undercommon, but preferred telepathic communication and would attempt to mentally dominate any non-slave, non-illithid they met. They fed on the brains of sentient creatures and were thus feared.'

One should note though that Dungeons & Dragons terms are only figurative in relation to the Nether. The creatures in the Nether and those in the board game are very different despite (thanks to the children in Indiana) sharing a name. The Flayer (to use the shortened version) is, as far as we can ascertain, what you might describe as the big boss of the Nether. Though little is known about this entity it is believed to be the orchestrator of most of the trouble that the Upside Down has inflicted upon our dimension. One could perhaps liken the creatures of the Nether to insects as a means to better understand them. The Flayer is the Queen Ant or Queen Bee in this analogy.

What we do know is that the Flayer is a persistent and dangerous entity. It doesn't like to beaten and will not stop until it has achieved its goals (the main goal of the entity appears to be domain over our dimension). The fact that the creature seems bent on conquest and despises humanity makes it a doubly grave threat. The Flayer appears to be a creature that is used to getting its own way. In one sense this is good because it means the entity may be prone to overconfidence, frustration, and anger - all of which are very human sort of weaknesses. Though a more complex and powerful foe than a mere stalking Demogorgon, the Flayer is not invincible and all is not automatically lost should you have to battle this entity.

The Mind Flayer is a malevolent entity that sometimes appears to resemble a huge spider monster seemingly made up of billowing clouds. This spider form is believed to be a proxy. The Flayer's spider form contains no discernible facial features. A unified description of this entity is impossible because it appears to be a shapeshifter which can alter its form constantly. We don't know what it really looks like and it could be that the creature is spectral in nature. It also, as we shall see, has remarkable and gruesome powers of genetic manipulation.

The Mind Flayer is capable of controlling the Upside Down creatures and vines - and also humans it comes into contact with. The entity has powerful psychic powers and so presents a considerably complex and three dimensional foe. The fact that the Flayer can control Demogorgons and use them as soldiers makes this entity nightmarishly dangerous to do battle with and defeat. It has been debated in scientific circles as to whether the Flayer has control over all the creatures of the Nether at all times. Some government scientists have proposed the theory that the Demorgorgon which stalked a small town in 1983 was in fact acting alone and not under any guidance or control.

This theory would obviously suggest that the Demogorgon captured the young boy and Miss Holland at random. However, academic opinion tends to counter this theory by asserting that the targeting of the boy was no accident and that the child was specifically chosen to be a manipulated spy for the Nether in our reality. One mystery concerning this theory though is that - if it is true - it doesn't really explain what the Flayer wanted with Miss Holland or why she was killed. As a consequence there is no verified or unified verdict regarding the lone Demogorgon and the extent to which it was controlled in its various activities.

One important thing to remember is that the Mind Flayer likes it cold. If you suspect anyone of being under the control of the Flayer then extreme heat (where applicable without endangering the life of the person in question) may be of use in driving out the possessed part of that person. It may also help if you attempt to rekindle pleasant old memories that person has and remind them of who they were before the Flayer took control. You must seek to bring forth the true personality of the possessed person and create the conditions where they can fight back against the mental control the Flayer has asserted.

The origin of the Flayer is unknown. We only know that the entity seeks dominion over whatever realm it discovers. There is evidence, as we have just alluded to, that prolonged exposure to the Nether leaves one with a psychic link to this mirror dimension. This was certainly the case with the trapped Nether boy. The boy spent a week in the Upside Down but when he was rescued he still experienced unsettling nightmare flashes where to all intents and purposes he felt as if he was back in the Nether. He was left with a lingering link to the Flayer which made him vulnerable to mind control and manipulation.

For this reason anyone who has spent a considerable amount of time in the Nether should be watched very closely. Though this might be difficult you must accept the fact that someone who has had prolonged exposure to the Nether may longer be completely trustworthy. They could well be working as a spy for the Nether and potentially place you and your friends in great danger if they are still being controlled. If you yourself spend a lengthy period inside the Nether you should make sure you are subject to medical checks - not just to ensure you are sound of body but also of mind. You should also ask your colleagues to watch you closely for any warning signs that you might have been infected by the Upside Down.

The way to severe this mental link is by closing the key energy gate (portal rift) which allows the Flayer access to our dimension. This is ultimately the only sure way to banish the threat of the Nether from your town should an infestation take place. By destroying or closing the main portal gate you should prevent the minions of the Nether from entering our dimension. Obviously though this is a task that is much harder to do in reality than it sounds on paper. As for other (smaller) dimensional rips, there is evidence that they might only be temporary. Test subject 011 successfully closed a gate in 1984 but one is highly unlikely to be able to find anyone with similar powers.

The best way to banish a Flayer from our dimension is to destroy the link between the Flayer and any possessed humans. This must be broken. If this is accomplished it should be difficult for the Flayer to maintain any presence in our dimension. If you are fortunate the gate might close of its own accord - in the fashion that the smaller Demogorgon portals tend to 'heal' and close up. This is - sadly - not something you can bank on though. The problem is that Nether related trouble can rarely be explained our own understanding of science. There is no textbook you can consult which will have all the answers.

The creatures and science (including portals) of the Upside Down are something we have yet to even begin to properly understand. Each new encounter with the Upside Down leaves us with more information to digest and (hopefully) learn from but the Nether still largely remains an enigma wrapped inside a puzzle. It is obviously not ideal for this volume to state that a portal gate must be closed to banish the Flayer but then offer only general and speculative ways to do this. I am afraid to say though that this is the state of affairs we reside under in relation to the Nether.

The key to the location of any main portal shall most likely be be the local government authorities in your jurisdiction. These government authorities will be of the covert and secretive variety. In all probability these are the people who will in possession of the main portal rift. There is a strong chance that these authorities may not necessarily want to close the rift. They may prefer to study and explore the Nether. This is an eventuality you must be prepared for. Government agencies of this kind do not like the public meddling in their affairs so you must be careful. You must be wary in your dealings with these people. If the events of Indiana are anything to go by then secret government agencies can be every bit as unpredictable and dangerous as the creatures of the Upside Down.

If the portal resides elsewhere then you can use a compass to find it. The electromagnetic field created by a dimensional portal will hijack your compass and lead you in its direction. Any portals you find should be closely guarded until such time as they (hopefully) heal up. As we have said many times in previous chapters, you are advised not to go through a portal unless it is absolutely necessary and unavoidable.

A government scientist is alleged to have proposed a theory that the creatures of the Upside Down are in fact alien beings from the Fourth Dimension who have infiltrated our world on a mission of conquest. It would appear strange to brand anything outlandishly preposterous given the facts we are discussing (alternate dimensions are nothing if not outlandish) but even in this volume (which, I daresay, some will choose to disbelieve) we must shoot this theory down in flames and consider it highly doubtful.

There is scientific credibility to the theory of alternate dimensions (and this scientific credibility existed even before the events in Indiana) but aliens from the Fourth Dimension rather veers us uncomfortably into the crackpot realms of David Icke rather than the more credible domain of Hugh Everett III. David Icke is most famous for the Reptilian Elite conspiracy theory. This conspiracy theory posits that the elites of the world are in reality blood drinking reptilians from another dimension disguised as human beings. The 'lizards' are supposedly behind influential and secretive groups like the Freemasons and the Illuminati.

David Icke is the most famous proponent of what is commonly known as the New World Order alien conspiracy. This, as the name suggests, argues that the elites (Illuminati) who run the world are actually not originally of this Earth. David Icke is far from the first person to write about this theory but few associated with this branch of conspiracy theory have become anywhere near as famous as Icke. One salient problem with David Icke's New World order alien conspiracy is that if these shapeshifting alien lizards have been meddling in human affairs for centuries then one would think that by now they would have actually set up the one world government they so famously (according to David Icke) want to establish. It is best to regard the reptilian elite theory as complete nonsense designed to sell books.

As for the possible existence of aliens and the chances that they have visited our planet, let us quote Francis Hitching on the subject - "Imagine, for a moment, that there are one million other civilisations in the Galaxy, all sending out starships. Since there must be something like 10 billion interesting places to visit (one tenth of all stars in the Galaxy), then each civilisation must launch 10,000 spaceships annually for only one to reach here every year. If every civilisation launches the more reasonable number of one starship annually, then we would expect to be visited once every 10,000 years. Human beings in general are great souvenir collectors. Yet of all the dozens of people who claim to have been aboard a flying saucer, not one has bothered to pick up the equivalent of a paperclip or a book of matches."

Despite the long odds, there are still regular sightings of strange lights and objects in the sky and claims by people that they have been abducted by little grey aliens. Many of the sky sightings can be dismissed as natural phenomena (satellites, shooting stars, aircraft, or even the planet Venus etc) that have been mistaken for UFOs but there are still many unexplained sightings that come from reliable eyewitnesses - like pilots and astronauts for instance. We know there are planets out there capable of sustaining life and it is possible they have technology way in advance of ours.

Could advanced spacefaring civilisations have mastered the art of bending time and space to make impossibly long voyages less impossible than they might seem? No one truly knows if we have been visited by aliens or not but if they did have the technology to visit our world then it is more than likely that they are able to do so secretly and therefore hide their presence from humanity. Have extraterrestrials visited Earth at different points in our history? Do they secretly confer with world governments? This field of study is a vast and an unfolding one that will probably never be conclusively solved one way or another - at least not until man explores the endless void of space for himself or those alien spacecraft appear in full view over the major cities of the world like they do in Hollywood films. The best advice is to keep watching the skies.

It is, as we have discussed, possible for a 'host' of the Flayer to fight back against the mental control exerted against them. This task is far from easy though and will take great reserves of willpower and concentration. The important thing though is that it can be done. Resistance to the Flayer is not impossible and that is encouraging. It is believed that the Flayer is able to establish a telepathic link with any creature or piece of matter - no matter how small - which finds itself in our reality. The Flayer can use this 'carrier' to control other creatures (be they animals or humans) and fuse them together into a new (and inevitably monstrous) form.

No matter how fragile and inconsequential the Flayer's presence in our dimension might seem it always has the ability to grow, dominate, control, and expand through the manipulation of minds and flesh. For this reason you should never take it for granted that the Flayer no longer presents an obvious threat or ever assume that it has been defeated for good. The Flayer is a patient enemy willing to bide its time and lick its wounds until it is ready to strike again. One must always be observant and be aware of any suspicious activity that corresponds to the modus operandi of the entity.

The Flayer can communicate through human hosts and is clearly an entity of intelligence who has no trouble absorbing information and memories in our dimension. The entity has the ability to quickly understand and speak human languages. It is not known what the true natural composition of the Flayer is. It can take the form of smoke and in this state often resembles a volcanic cloud. In its smoke form the mist of the Flayer can be controlled and used to attack and infiltrate a human host.

While we would classify Demogorgons as animal like the Flayer is more enigmatic and calculating and makes more use of strategy. This makes the entity a more formidable and complex foe than the native creatures of the Nether. The Flayer is a more supernatural sort of creature than the Demogorgon - which patently makes it even harder to understand and fight a battle against. The ultimate goal of the Flayer is difficult to say for certain but it seems logical to assume that the entity seeks to expand the Nether into our reality and make them all essentially one and the same - ruined and bleak.

The Nether appears to have a Hive Mind controlled by the Flayer. This 'possession' ability extends, as we have noted, to our reality if the entity is allowed to gain a foothold. The entity also has an obvious mastery of genetic manipulation. Should the Flayer ever gain a foothold in our dimension then it seems plausible to think that it would seek to exterminate the human race and take full control of our world. The Flayer appears to leech energy out of the dimensions it conquers. Should this entity ever be successful in its aims then our world would doubtless end up like the Nether and become derelict, decayed, and ruined.

Were the Flayer to take control of our own dimension it seems plausible to assume that our world would end up looking very much like the Nether. If you suspect that someone is under the control of the Flayer there are certain signs which may give them away. They will be cold to the touch and avoid the sun and heat. If you notice that someone suddenly refuses to go outside during warm days this may be indicative of Flayer possession. The eyes of those under the control of the Flayer might be dilated and they may have signs of prominent black veins or bruises on their body.

Those under the control of the Flayer can be highly dangerous and exhibit extraordinary strength in their possessed state. You should be well aware of this and always remember that a Flayer possessed person is more formidable than an ordinary human. The Flayer has been known to target specific individuals (as seems to have been the case with the trapped Nether boy). It is an entity who also always remembers key foes and targets them accordingly (the Flayer appeared, according to all data, to have harboured a personal grudge against test subject 011). The Flayer and those it controls are though vulnerable to fire and if you hurt the Flayer through fire the whole of the Nether will feel that pain because of its strong connective mental link.

Those who come under the control of the Flayer may find that the injuries they pick up while possessed do not heal in the fashion that injuries on a normal person eventually would. The Flayer appears to regard a host body to be disposable. It is a cold and emotionless entity indifferent to the fate of anything it encounters or controls. Because the body of a 'Flayed' person tends to end up with a lot of damage that doesn't heal in a normal way this makes becoming possessed by the Flayer very dangerous and hazardous.

Attempting to write a scientific journal or history of this entity frequently devolves into guess work because of our lack of information but some interesting academic essays have been written on this subject speculating that the Flayer is a creature who moves from dimension to dimension seizing control. This raises the possibility that there are many alternate realities which the Flayer has already vanquished. The only proven alternate reality though is the Nether which - as its more common name would suggest - appears to sit just below our own dimension. The Flayer sits just below what we know as reality and evidently casts envious eyes on our world. The Flayer is rather like a deranged dictator who keeps invading the countries next door to him.

There is speculation that the Flayer has the ability to manipulate the weather. This could be a consequence of the fact that it was alleged to emerge through storm clouds in 1984. It could be though that this was merely an illusion triggered in the mind of a connected human host. We simply don't know for sure if the Flayer can control weather systems but there is certainly evidence for the creature having the ability to adopt a mist like form and then control that mist so it gives the impression of a strong wind or hurricane. When it comes to the powers and abilities of the Flayer there is still much we don't know.

The Flayer is a formidable foe because of its ability to learn quickly how our dimension works. There is evidence that the Flayer can move through human memories and spy on people in an astral sort of way. The Flayer has patently learned a lot about our weapons, science, and military. The one positive note though is that this information flow goes both ways. If someone is possessed by the Flayer they will - should they emerge from the experience intact and alive - gather information about the Nether and the Flayer. Someone who has been connected to the Flayer but then managed to sever that link will be a valuable asset because they will now know more about the Upside Down.

There is evidence too that those who were once possessed by the Flayer have a lingering and vague connection which allows them to become aware when the Flayer is active in our dimension again. You might say that this works rather like the 'spider-sense' of Peter Parker. They should be aware of Flayer related danger before it actually happens. While this is a useful ability in a Nether crisis it should be noted that most of those who encountered the Flayer perished as a result of the experience.

There are vague scientific files (which were naturally highly classified) concerning an incident in 1985 where the Flayer used mind control to take command of an escalating number of people in the seemingly cursed Indiana town we have frequently mentioned. The victims in question did not survive this ordeal. The Flayer can command the creatures of the Nether and use them as soldiers. The DemoDogs which created so much trouble in Indiana in 1984 are believed to have been under the direct control of the Flayer. As we have noted though, if one is able to banish the Flayer back to its own dimension or damage the entity with fire then this should have the same effect on the DemoDogs or any other connected creatures of the Nether.

Remember that any action such as this will also have a harmful effect on any human controlled by the Flayer. You must make sure that the Flayer's connection to any human host has been banished before you take such extreme action. One frequent theory for the Upside Down is nuclear apocalypse. This is at the very least an explanation for why it looks desolate and abandoned in the Upside Down. It is a place of dust and despair and devoid of people - exactly what one might expect of a post apocalypse environment.

The explanation for the ravaged dimension in this theory would be that this is an alternate world where the Cold War went nuclear. This is a popular theory for a number of reasons. In 1983 the Cold War was still very real and the Upside Down version of this part of Indiana - by all accounts - does resemble the aftermath of a nuclear strike. The place is deserted, everything seems decayed and ruined, and there is dust and debris floating in the air. Cars are abandoned, buildings seem wrecked.

Those who go into the Upside Down wear Hazmat suits and scientists use radiation devices when they venture into this nightmarish world. Some exponents of this theory suggest that

Demogorgons are mutants who were once human. Maybe Demogorgons are what the survivors evolved into to survive in this hostile realm. How did the Nether boy survive in the Upside Down then in this toxic atmosphere? One explanation for that would be that this part of Indiana, as an out of the way sort of place, didn't bear the full brunt of a nuclear strike. Maybe some of the radiation levels subsided by the time he was trapped there.

There are some obvious problems with this theory though. It would be unlikely that Demogorgons could evolve from humans so quickly. Demogorgons seem more plant like than human in origin - the theory that they are fungi probably holds more weight than the theory that they are the survivors of radiated humans. One other problem with the nuclear theory is that it doesn't really explain the Mind Flayer creature. Maybe the Mind Flayer and Demogorgons are dimensional creatures who feasted on the bones of this ruined world but then become aware of our dimension - a place where food and prey is far more abundant.

A common scientific theory is that the Nether's life is essentially fungi. Fungi dislike heat and light and feed on decay. There is a theory that the Flayer may have created all the creatures that reside in the Upside Down. Given its mastery of genetic manipulation this theory is plausible but impossible to verify for certain. It is though, as we have noted, important to remember that everything in the mirror dimension seems to be biologically and mentally connected to the Flayer. If you can hurt or banish the Flayer then the other creatures of the Nether are much less of a problem.

The question of whether or not the Flayer created Demogorgons or merely conquered their dimension is impossible to answer with any degree of certainty. Such an answer would be purely academic anyway. We know that the Flayer controls the creatures of the Nether. How it came to assert this control is an interesting question but not one that has any significant relevance. There is an academic theory that the Flayer may in actuality be the human test subject 001. According to legend (government files on this case have mostly been shredded and are hard to come by) 001 was sent into the Upside Down by test subject 011 in 1979.

All available evidence suggests that 001 is not the Flayer but merely a powerful field marshal of the Flayer. 001 was named Vecna by the kids in Indiana who battled this entity. Vecna * was a wizard in Dungeons & Dragons. The character is known as the God of Secrets. According to a leaked file from the laboratory in Indiana where 001 resided, his real name was Henry Creel. He was the son of an infamous local killer named Victor Creel who was sent to an asylum for murdering his wife and two children. Henry did not die though. He had merely lapsed into a coma. It was Henry who had killed his mother and sister using his special abilities.

Henry was secretly taken into custody by the authorities at the lab - where he became 001 - but he proved to be dangerous and unstable. It was decided to place an inhibitor device in his neck so that he could no longer use his powers. He was given a new identity and forced to work at the lab as an orderly named Peter Ballard. Ballard eventually managed to trick test subject 011 into trusting him. He sowed distrust of the facility in her and encouraged 011 to escape. In return for this she removed the device from his neck using her powers. Though she had no way of knowing this, that act would have profoundly tragic consequences.

001 murdered all of the children in the lab - save for 011. She fought back and vanquished him with such fury it opened a rip to the Upside Down where Ballard was transformed into Vecna - most likely by the Flayer. This incident, if true, proves the theory that the first portal did not occur in 1983. Vecna preyed on victims in our dimension using physic links to these victims which induced hallucinations and nightmares. The MO of Vecna was to levitate victims and then snap all of their bones. The local police force was understandably baffled by the strange and gruesome nature of these deaths.

It is believed that test subject 011 played a part in defeating Vecna (just as she had defeated his human alter ego in 1979). Vecna's weakness, for those who to fight him without super powers, was that a connection to music could break the psychic he needed to establish with victims. A dossier on Victor Creel from the Pennhurst Asylum, indicated that Victor Creel believed that music playing on the radio saved him. Victor had no idea that his own son was responsible for

this awful tragedy. Victor believed his house had become possessed
by a demon. Should he still be alive in Pennhurst today, Victor
doubtless still believes that.

We should note that Vecna was attributed with having powers which
could manipulate time - which runs against the general theory that
time in the Nether correlates strictly to our dimension. Vecna could
make people in the Upside Down feel as if they had gone back in
time. We can speculate that he did this for the purpose of dredging
up bad memories. If something terrible happened to you in 1982 then
Vecna might well make you feel as if it was 1982 if you were in the
Upside Down. Vecna's murder sites in our reality would also open
rifts to the Nether. In this, the entity was similar to the Demogorgon.

One of Vecna's murder victims was killed in a lake - which led to a
rift opening at the bottom of this lake. This runs contrary to what we
assume about the Nether and its relation to water - although no
creatures came through the rift and out of the lake (whether the
Nether life took the chance to eat some fish is obviously unknown).
It would be safe to assume though that despite the presence of this
water gate that if one were to have gone through it then the mirror
dimension version of the lake would have been barren, dry, and
completely bereft of water.

To conclude our chapter on the Mind Flayer, it is impossible to
present a uniform description of the Flayer because it has proven
capable of taking many different forms and adapting to whatever
circumstances it finds itself in. The Flayer is estimated to have taken
control of around thirty people during an incident in 1985. The
ability of the creature to assemble a 'Flayed' army of human beings is
one of its most alarming and worrying abilities and something that
makes it very dangerous.

The Flayer can effectively create a new army for itself made up of
human hosts. The human hosts can infiltrate society because only
those with specific knowledge of the 'Flayed' and Nether related
science would be in any position to notice a difference in behaviour.
This is certainly a worrying scenario and one you should watch for
very carefully indeed. If you encounter the Flayer you will need to
have your wits about you at all times - even among those who appear

to be human.

* Vecna was first referenced in OD&D's third supplement, Eldritch Wizardry. 'Vecna was born as a human, centuries ago as a member of the untouchable caste in the Flan city of Fleeth on Oerth,' wrote ghwiki.greyparticle.com. 'He was initially trained by his mother, Mazell, in the arts of magic, before she was executed by the government of Fleeth for practising witchcraft. Vowing revenge, Vecna eventually assumed a mastery of the dark arts achieved by no mortal before or since. Some say this achievement was due to direct tutelage by Mok'slyk the Serpent, believed to be the personification of arcane magic itself.At some point during his long life and unlife, Vecna undertook arduous researches into the nature of life itself in a hidden temple buried in the mines near what is now Diamond Lake; the site of this laboratory is now known as the Dark Cathedral.

'Some nine hundred years after his birth, Vecna, now a lich and ruler of the Occluded Empire of Vecna, a great and terrible empire (in the Sheldomar Valley, centered near the modern-day Rushmoors) of the Flanaess, laid siege to the city of Fleeth with an army of arcane spellcasters and undead (VHotR). Legend has it that Vecna was nearly slain in this battle by clerics channeling the power of Pholtus, the god of light. The clerics unleashed a great burst of light, which hit Vecna primarily on his left side. Vecna was rescued and brought to safety by one of his wizard generals, a cambion named Acererak (who would one day himself become a mighty demilich).

'Vecna eventually recovered. On the verge of conquering Fleeth, certain citizens of the city came before him to beg for mercy. They offered up the entire city and her wealth if only Vecna would spare the lives of her citizens. When Vecna was not satisfied, the officials offered their own lives. Vecna gave one of their number, Artau, and his family, over to his lieutenant, Kas, who spent the entire day torturing and murdering them before the other officials. Still unsatisfied, Vecna slaughtered all within the city, and had their heads stacked before the officials, with those of their family members prominent. Vecna then granted his mercy, granting the officials leave to depart, and promising them his protection for the rest of their lives.

'At his empire's height, Vecna was betrayed and destroyed by his most trusted lieutenant, a human vampire called Kas the Bloody-Handed, using a magical sword that Vecna himself had crafted for him, now known as the Sword of Kas. Only his left hand and his eye survived the battle, perhaps because of the previous events in Fleeth. Vecna did not stay gone forever, and returned to Oerth as a demigod of magic and secrets.

'In 581 CY, his cult helped set events in motion that would have granted him the power of a greater god, but the plan was ultimately foiled. In 586 CY, Vecna ended up imprisoned in the demiplane of Ravenloft, but broke free in 591, emerging with the power of a greater god after absorbing the power of Iuz. Vecna then entered the city of Sigil, where he came perilously close to rearranging all existence to his whims. When Vecna was ejected from Sigil by a party of adventurers, Iuz was freed and Vecna returned to Oerth greatly reduced in power, though still a lesser god.' A 'lich' is an Old English word for an undead person. The word was used in the Lovecraft story The Thing on the Doorstep and obviously features in Dungeons & Dragons

TACTICS & TIPS

In the event of an Upside Down incident in your town which you have become aware of you should make use of C.B radio and also listen out for secret government or police transmissions (this is of course illegal under normal circumstances and only to be done in the event of a Nether related emergency). Ham radio is a popular hobby and makes use of the radio frequency spectrum for purposes of non-commercial exchange of messages. Ham radio can still be an important communication tool in times of crisis. The term 'ham' means 'amateur' as in amateur radio. In the days before instant global communication via the internet, telephones and radios were much more important. Amateur radio dates back to the 1890s and while used for recreation and fun has also been an important tool in a time of crisis or emergency.

'Amateur radio, also known as ham radio,' wrote searchmobilecomputing, 'is a hobby enjoyed by several hundred thousand people in the United States and by over a million people worldwide. Amateur radio operators call themselves "radio hams" or simply "hams." To become a radio ham, you must pass an examination. Wireless amateur communication is done on numerous bands (relatively narrow frequency segments) extending from 1.8 MHz (a wavelength of about 160 meters) upwards through several hundred gigahertz (wavelengths in the millimeter range). There are several license classes. The more privileges a class of license conveys, the more difficult is the examination that one must pass to obtain it.

'Amateur radio operation is fun, and that is one of the main reasons hams do it. But ham radio can provide communication during states of emergency. Ham radio works when all other services fail. After Hurricane Andrew struck South Florida in 1992, the utility grid was destroyed over hundreds of square miles. All cellular towers and antennas were blown down. Only amateur radio, the Citizens Radio Service ("Citizens Band"), and a few isolated pay phones with underground lines provided communication between the outside world and the public in the affected area.

'Amateur radio operators are known as technical innovators, and have been responsible for important discoveries. For example, in the early part of the 20th century, government officials believed that all the frequencies having wavelengths shorter than 200 meters (1.5 MHz) were useless for radio communications, so they restricted radio amateurs to these frequencies. It was not long before ham radio operators discovered the truth, and were communicating on a worldwide scale using low-power transmitters. Thus the shortwave radio era began.'

It is not advisable though to be too obvious in any snooping on government channels because they will be listening (or trying to at any rate) on you too. Make sure that you use codenames rather than real names when you communicate during an Upside Down crisis. If your identity becomes known to the authorities this could place you in great danger. At the very least you might be arrested and you'll obviously be of no use to your friends in a Nether crisis if you are behind bars. It would make sense to have special codes between you and your friends for when you discuss Nether related matters. This way anyone who is listening in will not know what you are directly talking about.

If you start openly talking about alternate dimensions and monsters then you are obviously going to expose the fact that you know about the Upside Down to any government agents listening in on the line. This is something you need to avoid. It is a matter of common-sense that you should be able to navigate around. You should watch carefully for any sign of police or government activity in a specific area during an Upside Down crisis. This might indicate where the real danger is located. Nether activity will (tragically but unavoidably) most likely lead to fatalities and so the police are likely to be the first on the scene when this happens.

There is no evidence though that the police and government authorities will necessarily be acting in unison. The chances are that they won't be allies. In fact, this type of incident (that is Nether activity) is usually what you might describe as above the pay grade of the police force. WAY above the pay grade. Even key government agencies were not told about the events in Indiana let alone the local police force. These matters are strictly on a need to know basis in secret government circles.

Secret government agencies dealing with situations like this tend to have a very low tolerance for any meddling and interference by the local police force. A Nether related incident will be dealt with by an ultra high security clearance branch of the government. The local police force would not be told what is really happening by government agents assigned to the case.

In the case of the Indiana incidents of the 1980s, the government authorities went to great lengths to frustrate a dual police investigation into the strange events happening in the town under siege from the Nether. It would be safe to say that they didn't appreciate a local police officer sticking his nose into their secret scientific and military affairs. The fact that this police officer was brave enough to investigate was very fortunate in the end because otherwise the boy would not have been rescued from the Nether. There is evidence that in 1986 two government departments - one scientific and one military - both competed against one another in an attempt to find the test subject 011. Suffice to say, these two groups were at loggerheads and there were even some reports of armed confrontations between them. Given the fact that government agencies don't even trust one another nor the police there is no reason to believe they will trust you either.

It may be for the best if you keep your distance from the authorities but this doesn't mean you shouldn't inform them of something that might be important. If you have information about a strange creature in our reality it might help if they are told. The government agencies will obviously want as few people to know about the Upside Down as possible. Only contact the authorities though in a worst case scenario. Only do this if you have no other options.

Dungeons and Dragons Dice

One must clarify that case studies relating to these scenarios only have the authorities in the United States as a guide. Secret government agencies in other nations may not act in the same fashion. They might be more trustworthy and kinder than the American authorities or they might be a lot worse. It will obviously all depend on where you are. If you live in a country that doesn't have a democratic system and leans towards stern dictatorship than you should probably avoid any government agencies altogether.

You should be very careful during a Nether crisis about divulging what you know to people outside of your circle of trusted friends and colleagues. If you tell someone outside of this circle the secrets of the Upside Down you may be placing them in danger. Keep the Nether on a need to know basis. Sometimes it is for the best if you don't tell those who aren't directly involved. Those who are ignorant or oblivious to the Upside Down will be of no interest to the government authorities and therefore safer. Ignorance really can be bliss when it comes to the Upside Down. You would obviously need to act to make sure friends and family are safe though. This does not necessarily mean telling them about the Nether. Simply make sure they don't go anywhere near where trouble might occur.

One obvious factor here is that if you tell someone about the Upside Down they are highly unlikely to believe you anyway. In a sense this a good thing but it could be a problem if you deem it important to bring a certain person into the fold (so to speak) but they predictably scoff at your tales of dark mirror dimensions and Demogorgons. In such a situation the only solution is let the person in question actually SEE something for themselves like a portal or Upside Down tunnel. They simply won't believe you until they have seen some actual evidence with their own eyes. Be careful though not to place this person in unnecessary danger. You will have a duty of care to anyone you bring into the fold. This sounds like a tricky balancing act for a very good reason because it IS a tricky balancing act.

The Indiana incident was complicated by the fact that a gang of children were secretly hiding test subject 011 after she escaped from the lab. This is why they conducted their search for the Nether boy without telling the authorities. They knew that the authorities would take 011 straight back to the lab if they knew where she was hiding and they didn't want that to happen. 011 obviously did not want to go back to the lab (her treatment at the lab was harsh and it wasn't an especially nice or normal place for a child to live) and the children were well aware of this and so sheltered her accordingly.

More to the point, the children knew that the local authority in question (The United States Department of Energy) had no interest in the rescue or welfare of their friend in the Nether (who the authorities clearly presumed must be dead anyway) and merely wanted 011 back. One would presume (and certainly hope) that the relevant authorities in a similar (but different case) would be considerably less heartless and much more helpful than the Indiana authorities when it comes to public safety or civilians trapped in the Nether. Ultimately, it is up to you to decide how much contact you do or do not have with local government authorities.

If you believe the government authorities be an impediment in the rescue of a friend you must give them a wide berth. You must be CERTAIN though before you take this course of action. There is an advantage to tackling the Upside Down from 'off the grid' (so to speak) but it will also leave you more exposed and make it more difficult to get the resources you might need. It may be that only the local government authorities have access to a main portal. This may be relevant to your quest. There might be a situation during a Nether crisis when you have to trespass in a government facility as part of your mission. If you choose to do this sort of activity 'off the grid' then you must make sure your preparation and strategy is thoroughly worked out beforehand.

It is important to note that no single nation has any ownership or exclusive rights to the Upside Down. The Nether is not a piece of real estate. It is not a piece of property that is owned by any single authority. It would be impossible to apply terms like this to the Upside Down. That would be like a nation on earth claiming they owned the moon and treating it like an overseas territory. It would be ludicrous. As far as we can tell the first breach concerning the Nether dimension took place in the United States but there is no reason why a rift couldn't open in another part of the world. As we have mentioned, there is considerable evidence that the Soviet authorities attempted to open a portal into the Nether on more than one occasion.

There are unsubstantiated and unverified reports that the Chinese military also conducted experiments designed to open a rift to the mirror dimension but we know little of the truth in this particular instance because secret scientific and military activity is even harder to uncover in China than it is in the United States. The difficulty in establishing any facts concerning China and the Nether is complicated by the fact that no consistent or unified conspiracy theory has emerged in relation to this matter. There are stories that the Chinese military attempted to access the Nether in Guizhou province but also contradictory tales that a portal was opened in Tibet by a Chinese version of 011.

We simply don't know if any of these alleged reports in relation to China have any truth and we didn't know if they successful in opening a doorway to the Nether. It would certainly not be surprising though to learn that Chinese agents and spies had learned of the existence of a mirror dimension and the Chinese authorities - like their Soviet counterparts - had conducted experiments designed to unlock the path to this parallel realm. The question of whether or not the Soviet authorities shared any of their knowledge of the Upside Down with the Chinese is an interesting one but impossible to know for sure. We can probably hazard a good educated guess though.

Though the two nations were supposedly communist allies the relationship between the Soviet Union and China was strained in the 1980s by the Soviet invasion of Afghanistan. It would appear doubtful then that - at this precise moment in history - the Soviet military establishment would willingly share a secret like the Nether with their Chinese counterparts. At the time China was not the economic giant it is today so it had considerably less leverage and financial superiority over the Soviet Union than the modern day China enjoys over the modern day Russia. It is highly doubtful that the Soviets would have shared their information regarding the Nether with anyone whatever the circumstances.

The attempts by the Soviets to access the Nether were always less likely to remain as secret and mysterious than any alleged Chinese activity because the Soviets were brazen (and foolish) enough to conduct a secret military and scientific operation in Indiana. Such a flagrant and hostile invasion of sovereign territory belonging to a rival nation indicated how desperate the Soviet leadership must have been to learn more about the mirror dimension. It was what you might describe as a reckless gamble. The Soviet version of Unternehmen Wacht am Rhein - albeit of a scientific fantastical bent.

It is just about plausible that wealthy nations with a high level of technological, scientific, or military expertise like (for example) France, Japan, Israel, or Great Britain may have conducted their own Nether experiments but there is certainly no evidence to prove that this ever happened. Though these nations are all allies and friends of the United States it is highly doubtful indeed that the American authorities ever shared any information concerning the Nether with them.

A team is vital in any battle against the forces of the Nether and constant communication will be paramount. You should all carry phones and even a back up in case the signals become blocked. Walkie-talkies are old-fashioned but worth considering as a back-up. Remember to use code for when you are explicitly referencing the Upside Down. The importance of a base property that can be well defended is also - as we have noted - vitally important. Should this house potentially come under siege it is advisable to cover the windows using nails and whatever wood you can find.

A Demogorgon is capable of breaking through a brick wall so be aware of this (the fortifications are merely designed to slow down the Demogorgon and will not be invincible) and make sure you stick together as a group. There is strength in numbers and a group of armed people in a room is going to pose more problems for a Demogorgon than a lone human in a more wide open space. A Demogorgon is capable of making short work of a group of people and this is where traps and fire come in. You must not allow the Demogorgon to get into full flow (so to speak). The most important thing is to come up with ways to slow the creature down and throw obstacles and distractions in its path. Only then will the creature become vulnerable and less effective.

Numbers are essential because, as we have noted, Demogorgons tend to hunt isolated people. There have been instances where a Demogorgon has attacked a group but this appears to have been more of an exception rather than the rule. Do not take refuge in a room with too much unnecessary clutter (clutter should be confined to traps laid directly in the path of the monster) because this will make it more difficult for you to move and escape. Remember (again) to make sure you have an escape plan and be prepared to make haste and flee at any time. Given the remarkable height and size of the Demogorgon it should be perfectly possible to come up with an escape route that a human being can enter but a Demogorgon can assuredly not.

Shotguns have proved to be quite effective against certain Nether creatures (the impact of a shotgun blast is alleged to throw a DemoDog back) but they do have the disadvantage of firing less ammunition than other weapons. Only use such a weapon if you are proficient and know what you are doing. Giving a potent weapon like a shotgun to someone who has never used a firearm before is obviously going to be rather pointless.

There is evidence of the existence of DemoBats. As the name suggests these are bat type creatures. In small numbers they pose no great threat but in larger groups they can be very dangerous. These bats are speculated to be spies for the Upside Down. You could say they are rather like drones of the Nether. DemoBats are most dangerous in a swarm. They also have a nasty bite. DemoBats are less sturdy than other Nether creatures though and can be dispatched by rudimentary weapons - like, for example, a plank of wood. If you encounter DemoBats you are advised to seek shelter and not stay in the open.

One can imagine that fire would be effective against DemoBats. Given their small size, speed, and ability to fly, it would probably be pointless to take on a swarm of these bats with a gun. Take refuge somewhere if you are threatened by DemoBats. If you can't get a building then seek to take cover in a dense woods. DemoBats are most effective in open ground so you should get out of any open land as quickly as possible if DemoBats threaten. It is unknown where DemoBats fit into the Demogorgon biology cycle - if they even fit in at all. It could be that they are completely unconnected creatures.

One government scientist suggested that DemoBats could be the culprits responsible for the Chupacabra cryptid mystery. Though an interesting theory the evidence is thin on the ground when it comes to verification of a Chupacabra/DemoBat connection. Sightings of the Chupacabra first emerged in Puerto Rico in the 1990s after reports that goats and sheep had been killed with vampire type puncture wounds and then had their blood drained. This local legend became more and more embellished and reported until Chupacabras had become a part of popular culture. But do these blood sucking rascals really exist? The problem with the Chupacabra mystery is that a fairly logical explanation for the animal killings and sightings of weird creatures was put forward by scientists a few years ago. They believe the fabled Chupacabras are merely wild dogs who have lost their fur through mange.

If you find yourself being stalked by Demogorgons or DemoDogs in an open expanse you should be cognisant of the fact that these creatures may use flanking movements in an attempt to surround you and create the conditions where they can pivot and strike at a more unexpected place. This is a standard human military tactic and also exists in the animal kingdom. Creatures once native to Earth like velociraptors are believed to have used the same flanking tactics when they hunted in a pack. Flanking is effective because it means the defenders may end up fighting on more than one front.

To avoid being outflanked you must retreat with all haste so that the creatures stalking you are essentially enveloping empty space. By doing this you are essentially retreating from a trap that has been designed to surround you and make you vulnerable. You are escaping from the noose before it can tightened. A flanking attack is basically one where the enemy creates a situation where they can attack you from the sides and then compromise your rear to the point where you may end up surrounded. This can be a very deadly strategy because one's focus is usually on what it is in front on you.

You are naturally more vulnerable to a dangerous side attack which you hadn't anticipated. In the case of an Upside Down infestation though you should assuredly be prepared for an attack from the sides. A flanking attack can create panic and confusion because the recipients of such an attack will find themselves suddenly having to defend themselves in all directions. This places them them in a much more dangerous and precarious situation. You must therefore expect the unexpected in such scenarios. If you are part of a team and do not manage to retreat in time to avoid being outlanked then make sure that your flanks are guarded and all sides of the team have at least one person assigned to them.

You must be ready to fight off any angle of attack in such a flanking situation. By doing this you take away the element of surprise the Demogorgons or DemoDogs had assumed they would have. Let us be clear though that you will still be in a most unwanted and perilous situation. If you do fall victim to a flanking strategy you will have no option but to fight tenaciously and seek to escape from the trap. Make sure you all stick together and both fight and escape as a team if this happens.

You should though, if possible, always seek to avoid fighting Demogorgons in wide open ground. Demogorgons are very quick once they hit their stride and they can leap long distances. Demogorgons are in their element fighting in open ground. They are less effective in constricted space - so long as you can stay out of range and throw as many obstacles, offensive strategies, and distractions in their direction.

If one is attempting to track a DemoDog or Demogorgon to ascertain its whereabouts or you want to lure one into a trap then using meat as bait has proven to be relatively successful. Demogorgons and DemoDogs will typically confine themselves to woodland in our reality. Their natural instinct is to reside in a place with plenty of cover. If you experience an Upside Down incident in a town surrounded by woodland or countryside you should be very careful and alert when you enter these areas - especially at night.

Do not make unnecessary noise in the woods and make sure that you have weapons and a flashlight. If you are going to have to enter the woods it would also make rather obvious sense to wear green and brown clothing so that you blend into the background more. We don't actually know how well Demogorgons can see or if they can even see at all but a degree of camouflage would certainly do no harm. Try not to wear anything that will reflect light. Take off jewelry and be aware that spectacles might also give you away by giving off light. Wear contact lenses if possible.

Try not to wear too many clothes and carry equipment that is too heavy because this will all simply tire you out and constrict one's movement. You shall need to be light on your feet and able to move fast at a moment's notice during a Nether crisis. Make sure that any bag or rucksack you have is very secure and will not snag you on anything. This is of particular importance if you are moving through woodland where there will be many branches, thorns, and bushes.

It might be advisable to invest in some infrared goggles at the outset of a Nether crisis as these are relatively cheap and highly useful at night. Night vision goggles use thermal imaging technology to capture infrared light. This way, you can see an image of what's going on in the dark. If you do not have any night vision goggles then spend some time outside in the dark before your night mission commences. Your eyes will take about thirty minutes to adjust to the dark and after this you will see much better - despite the fact it is night.

A good pair of binoculars should also be a part of your inventory in a Nether crisis. This will enable you to scan areas up ahead to look for potential danger or anything of interest. Binoculars are not terribly expensive and you should be able to purchase a competent pair without bankrupting yourself. An important tip in an Upside Down crisis is to always carry some stones or rocks in your pockets. These can be thrown as a distraction and piece of misdirection if you think a Demogorgon might be stalking you.

Do not carry keys, coins, or anything that will jangle or make noise if you are on an Upside Down related night mission. If you have a phone it should obviously be turned off during a stealth operation. An obvious but useful tip if you are being stalked by a Demogorgon in the woods and believe you won't be able to evade it on the ground is to climb up a tree, hide in the leaves, and stay as silent as possible.

If the Demogorgon should notice you in a tree and try and follow you up the tree you at least have the distinct advantage of being in an elevated position that is less exposed and easier to defend. It isn't an ideal situation but it is preferable to taking on a Demogorgon on the ground - where you would most likely stand little chance of survival. If you can create fire (alcohol, bandages, and a pole will suffice) then you should be able to ward the Demogorgon off. You main aim in such a scenario would be to injure or startle the creature sufficiently enough for it to retreat or take flight.

Setting fire to the creature or hitting it at point blank range with a powerful gun may do this although, as we have noted, fire is a surer bet against Demogorgons than guns. You will run the risk of setting fire to the tree but in such a grave situation this is a risk you must be willing to take. It is important to know the terrain you will have to use in the event of an Upside Down crisis. Ideally, you should already have a good local knowledge of any woods or areas you will operating in. If this is not the case do some research and consult maps. You are of no use whatsoever to your team if you keep getting lost and have no idea where you are half the time.

You must make sure that you always have a good grasp of the overall situation in relation to where your current location is and where any Nether related activity is happening. Remember to focus on the big picture in terms of strategy. You must keep track of the overall situation in relation to the town. If you do this the small details and little missions should take care of themselves. They won't be easy but at least you'll be operating under an overall grand plan.

You will assuredly need some wheels and transport in the event of an Upside Down crisis. Make sure at least one of you has a reliable car or van to ferry your team around to crisis points and important places. Bikes could also be very useful to get around short distances quickly and they can be used off road too. It is worth noting that if you become trapped in the Upside Down you should be able to find a bike somewhere and can use it to get around quicker. One should not expect any cars in the Nether to work though. They will be too derelict and the engines will be corroded.

If you are going to be spending time in the woods then long sleeves are essential because they offer some protection from thistles and branches and cover your skin - making you less visible. It goes without saying that you should use your ears in the woods and periodically stop and simply listen. If there are Demogorgons or DemoDogs in the area you may well hear them moving or pick up the distinctive and unique growls that herald their arrival. A good way to look for signs of danger in a woods or orchard is to get down on the floor and look around at ground level. If there is a Demogorgon in the vicinity then you will most likely see the feet of the creature from ground level.

When it comes to possession (that is to say a link to the Flayer) of those who have been in the Upside Down, there is a theory that this Nether connection is activated by the tendrils which make up a large part of the (decayed) flora and fungi of the mirror dimension. Victims of the Upside Down, as we have noted, have been found with one of these tendrils attached to them. There seems to be circumstantial evidence that if you avoid any contact with one of these tendrils then you won't be mentally connected to the Flayer if you make it back to our reality. Whether this is true or not we can't say for sure but it remains the case that contact with tendrils should be avoided for their toxicity alone.

It seems logical to speculate too that your chances of avoiding any residual mental link to the Nether are related to how much time you actually spend there. The less time you spend in the Nether the less likely you are to be profoundly affected by it. This is why we've placed great stress in this document on escaping from the Nether as quickly as you can should you find yourself there. If you can escape from the Nether in fairly swift fashion (which admittedly is no easy task) then you should, according to all available evidence, emerge in relatively good condition. If you do emerge from the Upside Down in short order make sure you take a shower or bath and also wash the clothes you were wearing thoroughly too.

During an Upside Down crisis it is vitally important to get some sleep when possible. Fatigue will be a big danger and you won't function or think as well as you should if you are tired all the time. Your reactions will be much better if you've had at least some sleep. You will be no use to anyone if you keep dozing off through lack of sleep.

Make sure you stay hydrated too by drinking plenty of water. You should also make sure you remember to eat. Make sure you eat plenty of fruit, nuts, and vegetables so that you have reserves of energy. Do not simply eat junk food.

It would make sense too to make sure you have some durable but comfortable footwear during a Nether crisis. An Upside Down crisis is likely to throw up many situations where you may have to run so make sure you have footwear that is easy and comfortable to run in while also offering some protection against wear and tear. It would be advisable for both yourself and your colleagues to come up with some agreed hand signals to use in situations where talking might give away your position to a Demogorgon. One can learn some sign language or military hand signals or simply come up with some simple ones of your own to all agree on.

Make sure that everyone is aware of what the signals mean and that you are all on the same page when it comes to these signals. There are instances where your greatest defence (in order to avoid detection) will be silence so hand signals could be very useful in an Upside Down scenario. In fact, in some circumstances they will be absolutely essential.

When moving through the woods, stealth is very important. Watch out for low hanging branches or pieces of wood on the ground because you will make a noise if you step on something or walk into a branch. Learn to walk toe to heel so that you make less noise.

In woodland it would be advisable to stick to footpaths because these will have less obstacles and things that would make a noise if you unexpectedly stepped on them. Be aware though that you might be more exposed on a footpath so be pragmatic in your route. If you get a sense that you need more cover then abandon the footpath. A flashlight is, as we have noted, essential but don't use it all the time because it will give your position away. Make sure too that you have some extra batteries for your flashlight.

If you notice your flashlight flickering or playing up or if the bulb suddenly pops then this could indicate that Nether activity has occurred in the vicinity. The arrival of a Demogorgon or the activities of a Vecna type entity would have this sort of effect. You should be on alert at all times but any unusual activity in relation to lights like this should put you on even higher guard.

Given the vulnerability of the Upside Down and its inhabitants to fire, this is an obvious weapon to harness but getting your hands on a flamethrower is obviously going to be nigh on impossible (and if you DO somehow get hold of a flamethrower please make sure that the person tasked with using it knows what they are doing or otherwise they are liable to set fire to themselves or a colleague). Molotov cocktails may be the simplest solution to the problem of harnessing fire as a weapon.

A Molotov cocktail is a glass bottle containing a flammable substance such as petrol (gasoline), alcohol, or a napalm-like mixture, and a source of ignition such as a burning cloth wick held in place by the bottle's stopper. Molotov cocktails may be effective in dispersing DemoDogs or halting the forward movement of a Demogorgon. It is certainly advisable to get hold of a gas mask in the event that you end up in the Upside Down. Gas masks are illegal in many jurisdictions but still fairly easy and cheap to get hold of. A gas mask filter in a decent mask will last for about ten hours and filter out harmful impurities in the air for much longer than that.

Gas masks are designed to protect one from chemical agents or radiation so they are very useful as a means to protect oneself in the Upside Down for a limited period (and one would obviously hope that you would only be trapped in the Nether for a limited span of time). Only use the gas mask though if you think you are in a relatively safe place and deem it absolutely necessary because your vision will be impaired inside the mask and you may not spot potential danger until it is too late.

We have mentioned the anecdotal evidence that the decayed flora of Upside Down tunnels seem to avoid water. There is also evidence of an incident where DemoDogs appeared to take evasive action when a sprinkler system was activated in a building in which they were rampaging. It could be that clean water is a foreign element to creatures of the Upside Down and one that they don't like it. It would be a stretch to propose that water is toxic to them (that would be simply too easy a solution and one that would have been discovered by scientists by now if true) but it is worth remembering that some creatures and plant life of the Upside Down do at least display what you might describe as an aversion to water.

It could be the case that if you were in a precarious situation a body of water might be somewhere that DemoDogs or Demogorgons might think twice following you into. In a desperate situation involving DemoDogs it could be that throwing yourself into water might be a plausible last resort (assuming of course that a body of water is close at hand).

We should note though that an underwater portal was located in Indiana in 1986 and there seems to be anecdotal evidence that tentacles from the other side of this portal were able to operate in the lake on our side of the breach.

The portal was allegedly opened because because a local school basketball player was killed in the lake by Vecna. It seems to be the case then that some creatures and plants of the Nether dislike water while other life forms in the Nether do not share this aversion and can operate in water. This makes data concerning water and the Upside Down complex and not uniform in nature. It all depends on which Nether entities or creatures you encounter.

We should note that the Nether entity who came to be known as Vecna seemed to prey on victims who were were struggling with depression or guilt. If you notice one of your friends or group members becoming distant and aloof or acting strangely (in that they seem distracted and react to things that aren't there) then you should watch them very carefully. Signs that someone has fallen under Vecna's 'curse' include nosebleeds and headaches. As we have established, music seems to be a significant mitigating factor to use against Vecna. If you suspect that you are being stalked by Vecna play a song that means a lot to you over and over again. A cherished song is rather akin to garlic and vampires when it comes to Vecna.

Given the toughness of vines and tendrils in the Nether it may be of value to carry a small hatchet or axe among your possessions in addition to a good quality knife. Not only would this make a viable last ditch weapon it will also be very handy in breaking free of any vines and creepers that try and trap you. Use as much force as you can on vines and tendrils because evidence suggests they are very tough and difficult to cut through. If you are snared by the foliage of the Nether you must try to escape from the grasp of this plant life as quickly as possible before your situation becomes more constrictive and any toxins are emitted by the plants.

When hiding during an Upside Down crisis it is important to make yourself as small and compact as possible. Make sure though that the position you hold is stable and comfortable and one from which you can take flight at a moment's notice (should you need to) without stumbling all over the place or making any unnecessary noise. When hiding you must control your breathing and seek to make as little noise as possible. If you feel as if you are about to sneeze it is advisable to stifle the sneeze if at all possible. Take some Antihistamine before any Upside Down related mission if you are prone to allergies. If you have an attack of hiccups (which will obviously give away your position) try holding your breath and swallowing. This often works as a cure for hiccups.

If you are going to use guns during an Upside Down crisis (and guns are certainly useful - though, as we have discussed, by no means a guarantee of success) then please make sure that anyone on your team who carries a gun knows how to use it. This seems like an obvious thing to say but it is very important. There is not much point giving a gun to someone who has never used a firearm before in their life and doesn't even know how to take the safety catch off or reload. It would make sense to undertake some regular target practice so that you have plenty of experience and know how to shoot, reload and aim with a reliable degree of competence. Always make sure that you keep the gun in a safe and secret place well away from any children who might live in the same house as you.

If you can get hold of any protective clothing it may be of some help to your in your battle against the Upside Down. A stab proof vest, for example, many not make you invulnerable (far from it) but it may provide some vital protection in the event of a claw slash from a Demogorgon or DemoDog. Make sure you have a good sturdy pair of gloves too. The more you can protect your skin from Nether related plants and creatures the better.

Evidence obtained by spies indicates that a Demogorgon can be held captive for an indefinite time but that it would take a prison type facility and military grade security in order to do this. It is highly unlikely that you would be able to do this as part of a civilian team and even if you did it would only be a very temporary measure. There were stories in U.S intelligence circles that the Soviets managed to contain a Demogorgon in a prison in 1986. The creature was occasionally let loose on inmates so that it could feed.

An even more remarkable claim is that the Soviets somehow managed to contain the Flayer. These stories are unverified though and impossible to investigate because Soviet documents from that era no longer exist. Attempts to locate this prison or talk to former members of staff may yield some results but as of yet no one has attempted to undertake this mission. It is highly doubtful that the contemporary Russian authorities (who now appear to be as unyielding and autocratic as their Soviet era counterparts) would welcome such an investigation or allow it to happen anyway. Russia is decidedly not a nation in which one should go snooping around looking for historic government secrets.

We have alluded several times to the fact that the creatures and portals of the Upside Down have proved vulnerable to telekenisis. Now, while this is a significant and welcome development, it is an unfortunate (or fortunate depending on your point of view) fact that very few people in the world have ever been proven to actually have these special abilities. There are though a number of people in the world who have developed what you might call super powers through MKUltra type experiments and lab testing.

The powers of these 'special' people are eclectic. They include abilities like the power to induce hallucinations or the ability to conjure fire (such an ability as the latter would obviously be a valuable asset in any fight against the Upside Down). We do not know how many of these special people there are in the world today because the files on them were highly classified and largely destroyed. We don't even know how many nations produced such people with special abilities.

As we have discussed, there is significant evidence that a secret government lab in Indiana produced a number of children with special abilities but most of these children were killed in 1979 by test subject 001 - who then became a Nether entity known as Vecna. There is no evidence that the lab replaced these children. Their focus seemed to reside thereafter solely on 011 - who was responsible for defeating 001. Should you learn of the existence of one of these people and find information on where they might be located it would make sense to try and recruit them to your cause. Their powers and abilities will give you a much better chance of defeating any Upside Down related trouble.

The most significant and important attribute they may provide is the ability to close a main portal gate. This would make them an invaluable asset. Be warned though that such an individual may not wish to be contacted and may also harbour a residual grudge against government authorities. You must ensure that any desire they have for revenge does not become a hindrance to your mission or threaten to sidetrack it. You must weigh up the usefulness of such an individual against how much much of a distraction they might be in a battle against the Upside Down.

All available evidence suggests though that anyone with powers of telekinisis or special abilities will be a fantastic addition to your team and could be the difference between success and failure. Not that you can't succeed without such a person - it will simply be more difficult. If you do locate someone with the ability to enter the mental void and track a person or even a Demogorgon then it may be of use to construct a sensory deprivation chamber for them so they can focus their powers with no distractions.

A sensory deprivation chamber can be constructed with a kiddie paddling pool, plenty of salt, and a blindfold. A paddling pool and blindfold are easy to get hold of but sufficient salt to float a person will be more problematic. One solution would be to break into your local government authority supply of salt to grit the roads in the winter. If you can find this stash of salt it should provide more than enough bags to be adequate for your needs.

There have been no other verified cases of Nether related trouble outside of Indiana although this doesn't mean that they haven't happened. Governments around the world have been known to keep secrets and cover up things that they don't want to be in the public realm. Those civilians who have been involved in mirror dimension trouble also tend to keep quiet about it and only share the secret with those who were also involved. This is for their own protection.

If you are aware of a Nether related incident it is obviously not wise to broadcast this to all and sundry because the government authorities may seek to silence you. Their standard tactic will be to discredit you. They could have you removed from your job or plant drugs on you. In most instances though government authorities will give you a stern warning before they take action. You will almost certainly be placed under surveillance - which will definitely curtail and complicate your Nether missions.

One of the most important things you must do during a Nether crisis is remain inconspicuous. You must seek, as far as you can, to be invisible to both the Nether world and the government authorities. Do not draw attention to yourself and if you are found near a government facility and questioned about this come up with a plausible answer that you can offer in such a scenario. Stealth and a low-profile should keep the government authorities off your back but - more importantly - may save your life if you encounter the forces of the Nether.

SURVIVING AN UPSIDE DOWN CRISIS

By now you should have the basic components in place to adopt a workable strategy in the case of an Upside Down incident in your town. It is worth going through now some of the lessons that we have hopefully learned in this document. The first lesson is that Nether related trouble is by no means an exact science. You must learn through experience when you battle the Upside Down and this is obviously something that is going to entail great risk to you and your friends. It is important not to worry too much if you experience fear during the crisis. Fear is a natural emotion and valuable too because it will keep you alert. Fear can also give you a strength that you didn't know you even had.

You must stay clam and clear headed during an Upside Down crisis because it is important to retain the ability to think straight. You will be of no use to your team if you become hysterical or too emotional. Focus on the task in hand and stay as composed as you can. If you do this your chances of survival will be much greater. Think of it in the following way - two boxers are in the ring and one is fighting on fear and flailing away in desperation while the other is calm and adhering to the strategy that they have spent months in the gym working on. Which of these two boxers do you think is most likely to prevail? The boxer fighting on fear will simply waste energy and forget the gameplan prepared by their trainer. The other boxer will be more precise and effective in their work because they are more relaxed and sticking to a plan.

One factor we should mention is that you must be very careful in the course of your Nether related investigations not to put innocent unsuspecting people in danger. If you are, for example, aware of the presence of a Demogorgon or DemoDogs then on no account should you lead the creatures into an area with a big civilian population. Creatures of the Nether are better contained in the woods or government buildings because they then pose less danger to the general public. Woodland or government property is also more likely to contain a portal - which is EXACTLY where you want the creatures of the Nether to head. Government properties will also have the resources of the military behind them and so will be better placed than you to engage in combat.

You have a duty of care during a Nether crisis to keep the general public as safe as you can. You must always adhere to this and make sure that no one on your team flouts this pledge and places unwitting civilians in danger through reckless conduct. If anyone on your team is consistently placing the public in danger then you must speak to them about this. You will either have to banish them from your team or assign them tasks where they are kept away from civilian areas. If any member of your team displays reckless behaviour then you must make sure that they are supervised at all times and not able to make any major decisions concerning your strategy.

As we have noted, there is considerable evidence that if the Flayer is banished back to the mirror dimension then this will also defeat the Nether creatures at large in our reality. Without the Flayer connection, the Nether creatures are rather like toys with no batteries or puppets without strings. The defeat of the Flayer should therefore be a priority in any battle against the forces of the Upside Down. If you can defeat the Flayer then the crisis should be contained - for now at least.

You should be aware that the Flayer is a very persistent and petulant adversary though and will bide its time waiting for when it can infiltrate our reality again. Even if the Flayer is defeated and banished back to the dark realm you must always be watchful for any suspicious or strange activity in your town. There is considerable evidence that the Flayer has a particular obsession with our dimension and has been angered by its inability to conquer us. This is doubtless an ancient entity that has been around for many centuries.

It is naturally the case that the existence of Vecna complicates our speculations about the Nether and its associated history and science. A retired intelligence agent - who must remain nameless - claimed Vecna was eventually defeated and no longer a threat. He was vague about the details and clearly not minded to be expansive in his answers. There is no reason not to take this former government employee at face value but all the same one should not take anything for granted.

As for the theory that the Flayer and Vecna are one and the same, this theory no longer has any credibility. They are separate entities and it would appear that the Flayer is the boss. It could be simply that the Flayer played a part in transforming the former Henry Creel into Vecna when he was banished into the Nether by 011. By now you should well aware that Vecna has a different modus operandi from the Flayer and as such you should be able to deduce the clues which will reveal which entity you are dealing

It is not beyond the realms of possibility that you may find yourself in a situation where both entities are active. This will be a grave and deadly situation requiring all of your fortitude and intelligence to master. It is said that the young Henry Creel had a fascination with spiders. If anyone in your team experiences hallucinations which involve spiders this could very well indicate that Vecna is active. Vecna is also said to use clock imagery to torment victims. If clocks feature in your nightmares this could be a sign that something is wrong.

By now you should be aware that even the tiniest trace of the Flayer in our reality poses a tremendous danger given its ability to rebuild itself and take control of living creatures to form a greater mass. This genetic manipulation makes the Flayer able to control human beings like puppets. Secret government files (which somehow escaped the great shredding paper purge) indicate that in 1985 the Flayer even used rats as a means of gaining a more concrete foothold in our reality. The rats were used to form a greater mass. With this in mind you should be very wary if you notice an unusually large swarm of rats in your area during a Nether crisis. There will be a good chance that they are being controlled by the Flayer.

The genetic manipulation abilities of the Flayer entity mean it can obviously do this humans too - not just rats. The important thing to know is that if you can break the link between the Flayer and all that it controls then you have won a major battle and perhaps even the war itself. Your ultimate goal in any Nether related crisis must be to block off the access between the mirror dimension and our reality. It is important to note that there seems to be a difference between a person who is possessed by the Flayer to be used as a spy (a double agent in our reality if you will) or those that have been irretrievably 'Flayed' (for want of a better term).

Those who have been 'Flayed' can end up simply as mindlessly violent and destructive. There is evidence that in 1985 two Flayed people tried to murder two teenagers in an Indiana hospital. A most brutal struggle followed but - happily - the two teenagers managed to survive. If you know for sure that a person has reached this tipping point and been Flayed beyond reason then no quarter must be given because they will try to kill you by any means at their disposal. You must forget who these people were in their ordinary lives before the Flayer seized control of them. They are now essentially zombies. If your life is threatened by a Flayed person in this condition you will have to stop them before they kill you.

It appears that a salient difference between the Flayed and those merely suffering a lingering mental link to the mirror dimension (which makes them vulnerable to possession) is that the former have been victims of genetic manipulation. They are too far gone to be saved and 'brought back' in the manner that possessed victims of the Nether evidently are. This is a determination though that can be exceptionally difficult to make. It is understandable that you might sway on the side of mercy and be highly reluctant to take extreme measures against a person who may have been Flayed. This will be doubly so if that person is someone you know. You must simply use your own judgement in such a scenario and be aware that if the person truly has been Flayed then they will potentially be highly dangerous.

By now you should be aware that the arrival of a Demogorgon is heralded by fluctuations in the power supply. If you notice lights suddenly flickering on and off then you should be immediately on guard and prepare for the worst. This does though give you a useful early warning system. It is important to remember too that those who have been exposed to the Nether but managed to survive tend to have a sixth sense when it comes to mirror dimension trouble in our reality. This is a very useful attribute to have and if you know of such a person they can potentially be of great assistance in alerting you to potential danger. The ability to sense danger before you stumble straight into it is an invaluable gift that may well save lives.

You must be aware that the seemingly supernatural abilities of the Flayer may make it feel at times that you are in over your head but you must always remember that this entity is far from invincible and has been beaten before. Even if things appear bleak and the battle is difficult you must stick to your task and do everything possible to vanquish this entity. Remember above all that the Flayer does not like heat. Though the creatures and entities of the Nether may seem unfathomable and supernatural, they all have a weakness. Fire can be used on the more prosaic (if one can call a Demogorgon prosaic) Nether creatures and mental control and discipline can be used to mitigate the threat of the Flayer and Vecna.

We have established by now that it is very unwise to directly confront a Demogorgon given their vastly superior strength and size compared to humans. Their dimension warping abilities can also make them formidable and unpredictable. You never quite know when a Demogorgon will strike and the element of surprise makes them highly dangerous. The ability to shrug off punishment and damage and keep moving forward is perhaps their greatest strength. Even if one were pumping bullets into a Demogorgon that was racing towards you it would be unlikely to stop the creature. You

will then have to be more creative in the way that you battle a
Demogorgon. You cannot simply shoot a Demogorgon.

Use traps, fire, and keep the Demogorgon distracted and confused as
much as you can. Tactical retreats are often necessary and nothing to
be ashamed of. A retreat means you live to fight another day. There
is no sense whatsoever in needlessly sacrificing yourself in a battle
that can't be won. It is often a pragmatic and perfectly logical course
of action to retreat. It goes without saying though that if a friend or
colleague's life is in danger from a Demogorgon then you must seek
to help them. In this scenario a retreat would reflect badly on you.

Once you have (hopefully) rescued your colleague (a temporary
distraction is probably your best bet to save a friend from a
Demogorgon) then you can take flight with your honour intact.
Always have the back of your friends in a Nether crisis. Your loyalty
and bravery will make them watch out for you too. If you ever get a
sense during a Nether crisis that one of your friends can't be trusted
or has become a liability then you must watch them carefully and
consider removing them from the group. You could perhaps find
way to engineer their duties so that they are no longer involved in
field work.

Demogorgons are reported to be as tall as nine feet. They tend to
crouch a lot but when the creature is unfurled and fully extends its
arms and legs it is an imposing and terrifying sight. As we noted, a
prison in the Soviet Union which once allegedly housed a
Demogorgon is said to have fed groups of prisoners to the creature in
order to keep it active and healthy. Whether this ghastly tale is an
urban myth or not is open to question but the story goes that a group
of prisoners were periodically locked in a courtyard with the monster
and given basic weapons like axes and knives. Once the monster was
uncaged the prisoners - according to legend - never lasted more than
a handful of minutes before they were slain in gruesome fashion.

Whether the Soviet prison story is true or not doesn't really matter.
The important thing is that it describes exactly what would really
happen if a group of people tried to fight a Demogorgon in a
courtyard with knives and axes. They would be completely wiped
out in a matter of minutes - perhaps even second. You must avoid a

similar scenario. Traps, fire, and an exit are all essentials for anyone who wishes to survive an encounter with a Demogorgon. Only engage a Demogorgon if you have created the conditions for these elements to come into play.

A government field agent once proposed that deep pits should be dug in the woods where a Demogorgon at large in our reality might hunt in order to capture the monster but it seems highly doubtful that a pit, however deep, would be able to contain a creature with the leaping abilities of a Demogorgon. Such a large and agile creature would surely find a way to get out of the pit. A scientific lab in Indiana reported in 1984 that DemoDogs proved to have excellent climbing abilities when they scaled a large wall from their subterranean Nether world up to the lab. It would appear logical to presume then that Demogorgons (who are basically DemoDogs at a more advanced stage of development) must share this natural ability to climb and scale obstacles. As such, it seems unrealistic to think that a Demogorgon would not be able to escape from a pit dug into the ground.

We noted earlier that hiding in a tree might be prudent if you are stalked by a Demogorgon in the woods and feel you have no way to evade the creature long enough to get out of the woods. The creature would doubtless be able to scale the tree if it knew you were up there but you would at least have a defendable position and the Demogorgon itself would be vulnerable and visible if it broke cover to try and get up to you. In such a scenario fire would be the best option to use but if this is impossible or you do not have time you would need a very good weapon to ward it off. A powerful gun or an axe. Some sort of spear might be useful in that situation.

If you do find yourself up a tree with a stalking Demogorgon in the vicinity then your main priority should obviously be to stay undetected. If you can use methods of distraction and lead the creature down a blind alley or other part of the forest this may - happily - enable you to avoid a confrontation. Throw a flare or throw a rock if you think you need to. Do anything you can to get the Demogorgon off your trail.

It is certainly not recommended that you retreat to any caves in an attempt to hide from a Demogorrgon. In such an environment you may become trapped and lose your bearings. Given that the Demogorgon is native to a murky dimension and has excellent senses it would seem logical to believe that the creature would considerably more at home in a cave than you and thus enjoy a distinct advantage in any such scenario. If you hide in a cave and the Demogorgon enters the cave then you would most likely have no way of getting out of the cave. Only go into a cave or tunnel network if you know these pathways well and know exactly how to get out them by an alternative route.

You must be flexible in your battles with the Nether. One must be ready to move at any time and - at the risk of repeating ourselves - don't be afraid to beat a tactical retreat if the odds seem weighted too heavily against you. There are certain situations though where flight may not be impossible. The life of a colleague might rest in your hands or you might have limited time to access a portal. In these situations you must simply do your best and try not to panic. Try to remember all the things you have learned about the Nether and its native creatures and think in strategic terms. These mental exercises will not only be conducive to your survival but they will also give you something to focus on and mitigate the anxiety you might (understandably) feel at being in such a difficult and tense situation.

You must be aware of the fact that if you end up in the Nether you may be trapped there indefinitely. There is no guarantee that you will find a way out. You can take encouragement from the fact though that at least three five people (and in all probability several more) have entered the Nether and lived to tell the tale. A trip to the Nether is dangerous and unpredictable but it is not necessarily a suicide mission. You must hold onto positive thoughts like this in the mirror dimension. Take heart from the fact that others have somehow survived in this awful place and managed to get out successfully. If you have face coverings, food, and water you should be able to survive in the Nether long enough to make a thorough and comprehensive search for a portal.

There are vague reports that a group of teenagers managed to survive in the Nether for a short time in 1986. They are believed to have escaped by making it to the site of a Vecna murder victim. They had deduced that this murder activity would leave a portal. Gravity in such a situation made it difficult to get through the portal (as it was located on a ceiling of all places) but they were able to improvise a solution to this puzzle.

One must remember that the Nether is not called the Upside Down for no reason. It is quite literally our reality - only upside down. It is right there beneath us but completely unseen. Logic dictates that the teenagers in question were able to use the lights as a means of communication to their friends on the other side (that is to say our reality). Given the awkward position of the portal some help would have been required for them to make it through safely back to our dimension.

If you find yourself inside the Nether you will literally feel as if you have been cast out to a hostile alien world. You will feel as if you are a million miles away from the comforting bric a brac of our own world. Take heart though in the knowledge that you are actually not that far away at all. In fact, you are right alongside our own reality and closer to home than you think. If you find a portal then you should (in most cases - ceiling gates and tough membranes notwithstanding) have no trouble in slipping back between the mirror dimension and our own reality.

Though your situation may seem grim and precarious inside the Nether take hope in knowledge that you are not really that far away from home. You simply have to find the door. That won't be easy but it is possible. Others have done this before and there is no reason why, with enough patience, fortitude, and effort, that you can't do the same. In such a scenario you must focus on the task in hand and remain calm and determined. Make sure you have all the neccessary supplies we have talked about and remember that stealth and silence will be your friends in the Nether dimension.

It may be valuable at this juncture to discuss a case known as the Montauk Project that may have some relevance to the events in Indiana. Montauk is a village at the east end of the Long Island peninsula. The Montauk Project is an escalating and strange conspiracy theory that revolves around the (now decommissioned) Montauk Air Force Station located in the area. The military presence in Montauk at this strategic point (it was remote with excellent observation of the sea) was first established during World War I. During the Second World War, the base at Montauk was named Camp Hero and home to all branches of the U.S armed forces - army, air force, navy. The military forces based at Montauk were charged with watching out for German U-boats and perhaps even signs of an invasion. The base was greatly expanded during World War 2 and acquired docks, hangers, and a torpedo testing facility.

When the conflict ended and Japan and Germany were defeated, the long tense Cold War with the Soviet Union began. A long range search radar (designed to watch out for Soviet incursions of American airspace) was built at the Montauk base in 1948. This structure would become one of the focal points for the conspiracy theories that would later abound in relation to the base at Montauk. The radar still stood after the base was closed, and, eerie and abandoned, dominates the skyline as one approaches the site. The base at Montauk was eventually closed in 1981 but even this fact is the subject a conspiracy - of sorts. The base was officially decommissioned by the military in the 1960s but is alleged to have remained active until the 1980s with secret funding and equally secret projects.

Theories about what had really gone on at Montauk (besides their official role of looking out for long range Soviet aircraft) soon began to venture forth, becoming more and more outlandish. They include teleportation, time travel, alien extraterrestrials, flying saucers, metahumans and experiments in special serums, the faked death of Nikola Tesla, the AIDS virus, bioengineering projects, and pyramids. So, as we can see, the conspiracy theories surrounding Camp Hero are very fantastical and to be taken with a generous pinch of salt.

However, one interesting fact about the base at Montauk is that, because it was decommissioned and abandoned, local kids with plenty of pluck and a camcorder were able to sneak into the facility and snoop around. What they did find was certainly strange. Not as strange as the more outlandish conspiracy theories but fascinating all the same. Weird electrical equipment and rooms with psychedelic wall patterns - something which evidently suggests that MKUltra experiments were carried out there with LSD. It could be that similar experiments took place in both Montauk and Indiana. Whether or not Montauk experienced any dimensional Nether trouble though is not known for sure. Some maintain that it did but we don't know the real truth.

The conspiracy theories surrounding the base Camp Hero kicked in with full effect in 1992 when Preston Nichols published his book The Montauk Project. In the book (which has a strange sort of introduction that invites us to regard the book as opening our 'consciousness' rather than cold hard fact that can always be backed up) we get details of Nichols' association with the base - which apparently came as something of a surprise to him as he had repressed his memories of Camp Hero. Nichols claimed in the book that when he visited the defunct base after it closed he met a homeless man who had been a technician there. The man told him that Nichols had been his boss at the base during a secret 'Project' which had incredible consequences.

Nichols then meets more people who claim to have worked under him at the base. His investigations unearth strange weather patterns in the village (snow in August, hurricanes), and animals behaving oddly. He meets a man who claimed to have been involved in the Philadelphia Experiment (an alleged 1943 experiment to make the USS Eldridge invisible to radar - this fantastical conspiracy theory alleges the ship became invisible and then 'teleported').

The book becomes increasingly 'far out' as Nichols talks of existing in different time spheres (to explain why he doesn't seem to know people who clearly know him) and even time shifts backwards to spend a day as the technical director of the base. He speaks of Project Rainbow, a stealth experiment which creates an alternate reality and enlists a Senator (who isn't named) to investigate why a decommissioned military base still functioned with no official source of funding. Nichols says his own theory is that the base was funded by Nazi gold secretly captured in World War 2.

The book further details experiments in reading a person's mind and time travel. Children were recruited for many experiments. It was no picnic for these kids though at Camp Hero. According to Nichols, a lot of them ended up shuttled to a ruined future. These were the kids you saw on milk cartons according to Nichols. They were officially missing but had really been kidnapped for missions at Montauk's secret facility.

'In addition to the derelicts, the researchers also used kids for some reason,' he writes. 'I'm not sure what exactly the purpose was. But there was one kid at Montauk who would go out and get other kids and bring them to the project. He was like a "tractor beam". He lived in Montauk and would circulate around very effectively. There was also an entire corps of these around the New York metro area that could get away for 6 hours-or-so without being missed. They were specifically trained to go out and bring in other kids. Some kids returned home, some didn't. The kids chosen were between 10 and 16. Or maybe 18 at the oldest and 9 at the youngest. Most were just about to reach puberty or had just finished it. They were usually blond, blue eyed, tall and light skinned. They fit the Aryan stereotype. To my knowledge, there were no girls in this group.

'A later investigation showed that Montauk had a NeoNazi connection and that the Nazis were still on the Aryan kick. We don't know where the kids went, what they were educated in or programmed for. Whether they came back or not is still a mystery. What information is available is that they sent every raw recruit into the Future to 6037 AD, always to the same point to what appeared to be a dead city in ruins. Everything was stationary, not unlike a dream-like state. There were no signs of life. In the centre of the city was a square with a gold horse on a pedestal. There were inscriptions on that pedestal and recruits were sent there to read what they said. Each recruit would interpret and report.'

Nichols' book becomes increasingly outlandish as it continues on. He talks about a mission to the pyramids of Mars using a 'vortex' that could be walked through. The book cites the mock documentary Alternative 3 (which is about elites secretly escaping to Mars because they know that Earth is doomed - us poor undertrodden folk will of course be left behind to perish) as if Alternative 3 is evidence for a colony on Mars. Nichols is seemingly unaware that Alternative 3 was a famous hoax.

Naturally, there is a monster in the book. Nichols says that a physic named 'Duncan' released a monster from his subconscious during an experiment that created a time paradox (with no less than two different versions of Duncan appearing in the time travel chaos). 'We finally decided we'd had enough of the whole experiment. The contingency program was activated by someone approaching Duncan while he was in the chair and simply whispering "The time is now". At this moment, he let loose a monster from his subconscious. And the transmitter actually portrayed a hairy monster. It was big, hairy, hungry and nasty. But it didn't appear underground in the null point.

'It showed up somewhere on the base. It would eat anything it could find. And it smashed everything in sight. Several different people saw it, but almost everyone described a different beast. It was either 9 feet tall or 30 feet tall depending on who saw it. I personally believe it was about 9-or-10 feet in height. Fright does strange things to people, and no one was sure of what the exact physical constitution of this monster was. No one was in any frame of mind to calmly and collectively analyse its exact nature.' Could this monster be the inspiration for the Demogorgon? The book includes a most unconvincing and inclusive (not to mention murky) black and white photograph of the alleged beast.

'After the events of August 12, 1983,' writes Nichols, 'the Montauk Air Force Base was abandoned. By the end of that year, there was no knowledge of anyone being on the base. In May or June of 1984, a crack squad of Black Berets were sent to the base. I believe they were Marines but I'm not absolutely sure. They were reportedly ordered to shoot anything that moved. Their purpose was to purge anyone who might be on the base. There was a second team that followed the Black Berets. They removed secret equipment which was considered too sensitive to leave behind. The next step was to prepare the underground to be sealed. Certain incriminating evidence was removed at this point. I've heard that a room with hundreds of skeletons was cleared out during this evolution. About 6 months later, a caravan of cement mixers appeared on the base. Many people saw these trucks. They filled the vast underground areas of Montauk with cement. This included dumping cement down the elevator shafts as well. The gates were locked up, and the base was abandoned for good.

'If one travels to Montauk Point today and parks in the state parking lot near the light house, it is possible to get a good view of the giant radar reflector that sits atop the transmitter building. For those who are either brave or foolish, one can follow the dirt roads that lead to the base. Most of the entrance gates have been bent or otherwise vandalized so that entrance is easy. This was probably done by local juveniles who sometimes get drunk and have beer parties on the base.

However, walking on the base is prohibited by New York State park rangers who periodically patrol the area. There are also occupied buildings on the main roads to the base. It should be noted that I am not writing this information to lure people to the base. People are going to be curious after reading this book, and it is my responsibility to warn them.

'I'm not absolutely sure of the legal technicalities. But walking on the base is probably illegal. One goes at one's own risk. [The entirety of Fort Hero including the inner Montauk Base has since been donated to New York State as a park. While there are peculiar political arrangements concerning the base to this day, the rangers are not out of bounds in keeping people off the grounds. The buildings are in a state of disrepair and are potentially dangerous to those going on a casual walk.] There are also other dangers to consider. Two people I know who participated in the Montauk Project visited the area in the late 80s. They claimed they were abducted and do not totally remember what happened to them. Another person has reported in August of 1991 that video cameras can now be seen from the top of the transmitter building. This is a new development and is rather odd considering it is a vacant and derelict facility.'

The Montauk mystery (if we can call it that) is an interesting sort of conspiracy with many elements that evoke the Nether intrigue. While most of the conspiracy theories linked to Camp Hero are preposterous and fictional and were designed to sell books, there are certainly a few unanswered questions and clearly something secret was going on - even if it probably wasn't anywhere near as fantastical as the more fanciful claims of Nichols.

Could there be a connection between the events at Montauk and those in Indiana? It has been suggested that similar top secret government experiments took place in both areas and disinformation was used to disguise what really happened at Montauk. In this scenario Preston Nichols would essentially be a fictional character created to discredit the strange goings on in Montauk. Governments often use disinformation to distract attention. It could be that some of the same scientists worked at both the lab in Indiana and at Camp Hero.

One can easily see which parts of the Montauk legend might be fabricated to muddy the waters. Time travel and jaunts to other planets feel like obvious embellishments designed to take credibility away from the stories pertaining to Camp Hero. However, we know from the events in Indiana that rifts to other dimensions can be opened so it seems plausible that something similar happened in Montauk. This would explain why parts of the base there are still fenced off and guarded. It is recommended that as part of your research for battling the Nether you should read up on the Montauk conspiracy. Parts of the legend of Camp Hero may well be relevant in fighting the Upside Down.

The village of Montauk wasn't quite finished yet when it came to mysteries though. It dredged up (quite literally) a further mystery to add to its rather mysterious legend in the form of the Montauk Monster - an unexplained creature who washed up on the shore on beaches near Montauk Point on New York's Long Island.. Photographs of said beast rather anticipated (or perhaps echoed) the DemoDog creatures which showed up in Indiana in 1984. The creatures were taken away by the authorities - though not before they attracted a lot of local interest. To this end a disinformation campaign was launched which dismissed the washed up creatures as raccoons or something along those lines. Were these creatures really from the Nether? It is hard to say though conspiracy theorists suspect that Plum Island may have had something to do with this mystery.

Plum Island Animal Disease Center was a secret government agency and located a couple of miles off the coast of Long Island. The base of the Disease Center was known as Building 257. This is where research into animal viruses took place. The original Building 257 is a stark and functional white block that looks rather like a factory block. Conspiracies have naturally flourished in relation to Plum Island and many of these are far more credible than some of the fanciful conspiracies linked to Camp Hero. Secret documents have suggested that Plum Island was secretly used for biological weapons research. It was even alleged that Lyme Disease was created at Plum Island as a bioweapon - although this theory was debunked when it was established that Lyme Disease was endemic before the facility on Plum Island was created.

The biological experiments at Plum Island ended in 1969. The island is still said to be toxic though as a result of all the research that went on there. It is believed that captured Nazi scientists might have worked at the facility on Plum Island and germ warfare research may have been undertaken. Plum Island is exactly the sort of place where Nether intrigue might feasibly abound. Brookhaven National Laboratory (in Upton, NY) is another facility that could have experienced Nether trouble. This lab is owned by the U.S. Department of Energy and most definitely not open to the public. It engages in all manner of remarkable scientific experiments and has a Relativistic Heavy Ion Collider which is used to learn more about dark matter and the nature of the universe. It's safe to say though that the research at Brookhaven is considerably less grim than what went on at Plum Island.

You should be well aware by now that the Flayer seems to control the extensive vine system which festoons the Nether. You should be well aware that the Nether's dangers include not just its creatures but also its decayed plant life. Fire is an effective way to keep these plants at bay. Make sure that you never allow a tendril or Nether tentacle to get too close to you. If if does you must use a knife or axe to free yourself and get rid of the attacking plant. Do not make the mistake of underestimating or even forgetting how dangerous the plants of the mirror dimension can be.

The toxic pollen these plants can dispense is highly debilitating though apparently not necessarily fatal. If you are sprayed with this pollen you may become unconscious. This is why face protection is so important. If you wake up after being poisoned by this substance try and wash your face with water as fast as you can. You should take heart from the fact that while the creatures of the Nether are cunning they are not infallible. They can be outsmarted. If you are well prepared and adopt the tactics we have discussed in this document then there is no reason why you can't survive encounters with Demogorgons and DemoDogs.

The important thing to remember is not to be too reckless. You must use stealth and caution and know when to go on the offensive and when to lay low. The fashion in which you juggle these tactics will be the key to victory or indeed defeat. Should you find yourself trapped in a facility with Nether creatures make sure that you move quietly and don't rush around corners without checking to see what might be around them. Cleaning cupboards make good places to hide in an emergency. The Flayer certainly presents a more formidable challenge than Demogorgons and is highly intelligent (with the capacity to absorb information about our dimension and use this information against us) but the Flayer is by no means unbeatable.

The Flayer was defeated twice in Indiana when it attempted to gain a foothold in our reality. If you are brave enough and (crucially) smart enough then there is no reason why you can't ultimately defeat the Flayer too. There is certainly enough evidence to suggest that the Flayer can become overconfident. The Flayer seemed to develop a vendetta against test subject 011 - most likely because it deduced she had the power to threaten him. This suggests that the Flayer can become distracted. One should remember that if you encounter a group of Flayed people they are mentally connected. This means if you damage one of them the others will also be damaged. The mental connection of the Flayed can be a strength but it is also a weakness you can exploit.

The question of why the boy survived an encounter with the Demogorgon but Miss Holland did not has led to a theory that it may be because the Demogorgon was under the control of the Flayer when it kidnapped the boy and transplanted him into the Nether. The theory suggests that the Flayer wanted a human host for a spying mission in our dimension and the boy was used as that spy. Miss Holland was patently not spared nor used as a spy but whether this all was by design or accident is impossible to say for sure. It could be that the Demogorgon was not under the control of the Flayer at the time and simply killed Miss Holland in accordance with its hunting instincts.

It is worth noting that despite the theory that the Demogorgon and Nether creatures and flora are wary of water this would appear to be contradicted by the fact that Miss Holland was attacked by the Demogorgon while sitting on the diving board of a swimming pool. However, evidence suggests that a Demogorgon attack could involve dimensional warping. In other words, the attack on Miss Holland would most likely have dragged her into the Nether version of the swimming pool - which definitely would NOT have contained water just as the Nether version of the lake in Indiana where some teenagers ended up in 1986 most likely did not contain any water.

In your dealings with Nether related activity please remember that anyone who has been controlled or linked with the Flayer will feel pain if you burn Nether related vines and material. Bear this in mind - especially if the affected person is a friend. You will need to banish the Flayer's control over them before you take measures like this otherwise you will just be harming that person. A good way to understand the Flayer is to think of it as an intelligent virus. You must remember too that the electromagnetic field allows one to manipulate electrical items between dimensions. If you pick up a phone in the Upside Down then static will be heard in the parallel phone in our dimension.

The rules of the Nether are not entirely consistent but you can take heart from the fact that there do seem to be ways to communicate from the mirror dimension. If you can't find a portal and feel as if your situation has become desperate then you must consider attempting this form of communication - be it through telephones or lights. Regarding Demogorgon biology, it is unknown if the insides of the creature are more vulnerable than the outside - though one would presume they MUST be. We simply don't know for sure though. The creature's biology is clearly designed to make it as tough and durable as possible. It is exceptionally difficult to fatally injure a Demogorgon but it is possible to throw the creature off balance with enough force.

Those who have encountered a Demogorgon but lived to tell the tale have suggested that the monster's scaly skin appears almost rock like up close. Demogorgons can be injured but it would take a considerable amount of firepower to damage its exterior and even then the creature has self-healing abilities. Reports indicate that the Demogorgon - though an implacable predator - will beat a tactical retreat if it considers such a course of action prudent. It is only in extreme situations though where the creature will do this. If you, for example, subject the Demogorgon to fire it may decide to go away and wait for a fresh chance to attack. Though scientific circles tend to think of Demogorgons as instinctive feral creatures they have shown they can be patient and make tactical decisions.

One tactic that is worth considering (though it is obviously a dangerous tactic because it will require close proximity to the monster) is to throw something like a Molotov cocktail or firework into the mouth of the Demogorgon when it opens. This may not kill the creature but it will distract and distress the beast long enough for you to escape or adopt stronger tactics. Throwing a device like this into the mouth of a Flayer monster is also a tactic worth considering.

From what we know of Nether creatures, explosives and fire tend to work against them better than bullets. Given the plant like qualities of the Demogorgon is is not really known if bullets would actually kill the creature. There have been no reported incidents of a bullets felling a Demogorgon. The same isn't quite the case for DemoDogs. As we have noted, it is believed that DemoDogs can be thrown back more forcibly by gunfire - especially it comes from a high impact weapon like a shotgun.

The Demogorgon has been known to bleed but the loss of this sap like liquid did not appear to slow up the beast very much. An incident in Indiana where the creature was caught in a bear trap had no long lasting effect - which is most likely (in addition to the creature apparently recovering from being set on fire) where the theory that the Demogorgon has regenerating health comes in. In essence then we are dealing with a creature that probably can't be killed by conventional means (bullets) but it would be plausible to assume that high concentrations of explosives would do potentially fatal damage. This is obviously though something you should only do if you have someone trained in this field and you deploy the explosives in a place that won't endanger the public.

One military expert has suggested that throwing a grenade in the Demogorgon's mouth would almost certainly incapacitate and probably kill the creature. Such a course of action would most likely be effective at stopping the Demogorgon but one would have to be very close to the monster to ensure the aim was true and in doing this you obviously place yourself in great danger not just from the Demogorgon but also the blast radius from the grenade.

The blast would most likely be partly contained by the thick hide of the Demogorgon's skin but some effect would still be felt and there is the obvious of missing the target and thus sending a live grenade into an open space in which you reside. The chances of a civilian getting hold of a hand grenade in the first place though are admittedly quite remote. Only someone with a professional military background should consider messing around with hand grenades.

You should be aware by now that Demogorgons are surprisingly fast. They can run on all fours and have been known to vanish from the scene in no time at all. There is evidence that they have some climbing skills and also have the ability to cling to a ceiling in order to pounce on prey. A government field agent who was present at a 1983 incident involving a Demogorgon at a lab wrote a detailed report of which only partial fragments remain. The agent survived the encounter because he was positioned in another corridor to the Demogorgon attack and so watched from afar. The relevant section of what remains of his report makes for illuminating reading.

'The creature appeared suddenly in the light strobed corridor and almost instantly the lights went haywire - as if a great surge of incredible power had washed through them and then vanished. They flickered for a few minutes and then the corridor was dark save for the flashes of gunfire. Several armed military police officers found themselves in the eye of the storm and machine guns crackled away. The sound of gunfire quickly gave way to the sound of screaming. The armed M.P.s were slaughtered by the creature in what seemed like a matter of seconds. I could see bodies and blood on the floor whenever the lights flickered and then all would go dark again. This repeated several times - each successive flash of light revealing more blood and more victims.

'The creature stood at least seven foot and had arms that seemed big for its body. The creature's hands were huge and had powerful looking claws at the end of each finger. Though I did not see the carnage in perfect detail I could make out enough to see that the creature's claws were its chief weapon and responsible for the dreadful slaughter now happening only a corridor away. The creature was light in skin tone - a sort of milky brown - and surprisingly light on its feet given the incredible mass of weight and muscle it carried. The head of the monster was most disconcerting for it had no face. The head opened up to reveal nothing but teeth. Most terrifying of all was the high pitched roar of the beast as it killed the military employees. Somewhere between a roar of pleasure and a cathartic scream, the sound was curiously unsettling as it seemed to indicate that the monster was enjoying its work. My own conjecture, which I accept has not been popular, is that this sound was the monster's version of a cat purring.'

Much of the agent's report is missing so we don't know the precise details on how he managed to escape from the monster. We can only presume that the Demogorgon was preoccupied killing the other agents and then sloped off to another part of the building - leaving the agent alive. It would be safe to assume that if the Demogorgon had noticed the agent and pursued him then this agent would not have lived to write a report about this incident.

Residue and radition is left at the scene when a Demogorgon teleports. This is important to remember. If you see slime like residue at a site it may indicate that a Demogorgon has been here. It may be wise to invest in a Geiger counter so that you can check for radiation in such scenarios. This should confirm whether or not a Demogorgon has been here.

The radiation appears to be a by product of the creature using dimensional portals to travel. It is recommended that if you do come across evidence of Demogorgon residue that you do not touch anything and try to keep your distance.

Make sure you have at least a face covering and gloves if you investigate anything that you think may be a Demogorgon teleportation site. Ideally you should really have a hazmat suit but, as we have noted, these are not exactly a common wardrobe staple for civilians. It is obviously not advised that you go anywhere too near radiation - even if it constitutes a very small amount.

A high ranking military officer once proposed that in order to vanquish the threat of the Nether once and for all a nuclear bomb set be set off in the mirror dimension. It is believed that the officer in question (who was speculated to be a Lt. Colonel) was deadly serious when he proposed this. The main problem with this idea is that we have no idea if it would actually work. What if the mirror dimension survived a nuclear blast? What if it made no difference? If the mirror dimension is a facsimile of our own world in scale then even a nuclear bomb isn't going to destroy everything. If one were to destroy New York with a nuclear bomb the rest of the United States and the rest of world would still be there. The same would be true of the Upside Down.

We also have no way of knowing what effect a nuclear blast in the mirror dimension would have on our own reality. Such an extreme course of action would simply have too many unknown variables. A nuclear blast might create enough energy to close a portal gate but what if the energy triggered a cataclysm which affected our own dimension? We also suspect that the Flayer controls multiple dimensions so it might simply move anyway and avoid the nuclear blast. Besides, the Flayer has been defeated before without resorting to such drastic measures.

What if the nuclear blast created many new dimensional gates or one gigantic dimensional gate between the two known realities? If may sound fantastical but we simply don't know what effect a nuclear detonation in the Upside Down would have. Let us hope that the more hawkish voices in the military are never allowed to gain any traction with the theory that nuclear weapons might somehow destroy the Nether once and for all. It is a gamble that is not worth risking. The nuclear option - you might say at the risk of a bad pun.

A first-aid kit should be an essential part of your supplies in the event of a Nether crisis but it would also be prudent to have a first aid booklet or book on you. Ideally you will have studied this material. You must know how to apply bandages and treat wounds. Part of your duties may involve having to treat someone who is suffering from shock. According to wikihow.com - 'Shock is the inadequate flow of blood to the vital tissues and organs. If untreated, it can be fatal. Shock results from excessive blood loss, deep burns, or reactions to the sight of a wound or blood. The signs are restlessness, thirst, pale skin and rapid heartbeat. Sweating may occur even if the skin feels cool and clammy. As it worsens, they breathe short fast gasps, with a vacant stare. To treat: maintain proper heartbeat and respiration by massaging the chest and positioning the person for adequate respiration. Loosen any constrictive clothing and reassure the person. Be firm yet gentle with self confidence.'

As we have noted, a proven way to defeat the Flayer is to tap into the memories of those people it has taken control of. If you can remind them of happy memories and who they once were this will encourage Flayed people to fight back against their mental link to the Nether. If you do this you can destroy any power the Flayer has in our dimension by breaking his connection to these human possessed avatars. The most encouraging thing about this strategy is that it doesn't require the power of telekenisis nor a nuclear device (two things which you are obviously highly unlikely ever to have access to). This strategy is your most plausible way to defeat the Flayer because it won't require resources you may not have. The only thing it will require is past knowledge of the life of a Flayed person.

It is entirely possible that in the course of your dealings with the Nether that you may come across a creature from the mirror dimension that no one has encountered yet and so is unclassified and a beast we have no information on at all. It stands to reason that there MUST be creatures in the Nether we have not seen yet. Who knows how many different species there might be in the mirror dimension? Given you will have no knowledge about how this new creature operates or what its strengths, weaknesses and abilities are in such a scenario you should tread very carefully and not rush into any confrontation with the unknown species.

Keep your distance from any unclassified creatures until such time as you've built up more information about them. Study their behaviour and movements and log any abilities they may have. One should also attempt to deduce if any new creature has the ability to teleport and drag humans into the Nether. It would appear that Demogorgons are the most common creature of the Nether but be prepared for the unexpected because you may end encountering a monster that no human being has ever met before.

It is not recommended that you attempt to use poisons in an attempt to combat the creatures of the Upside Down. There is no evidence that such a strategy would have any effect and you would simply be placing yourself in danger by handling hazardous chemicals. Given that the atmosphere of the Nether is very toxic it stands to reason that - in all probability - the life in this mirror dimension would have a strong immunity to any toxic substances from our own (far less inhospitable) dimension.

There is no evidence that the military and scientific establishment have ever used poisons or chemicals to fight the Nether world - which tells you all you need to know about the logic of this approach. Their defensive weapon of choice is fire. Fire is the only weapon proven to have a tangible effect on the Nether world.

MISCELLANEOUS

Remember that you may - if you are unfortunate enough to spend time in the murky and danger strewn depths of the Upside Down - experience a number of small earthquakes and palpable ground tremors in this strange dimension. Why these tremors and disturbances occur has not been established by scientists but it would seem logical to suggest that they may arise as a result of instability caused by the opening of dimensional gates. The opening of gates invokes a tremendous surge of energy. If this theory is correct then the instability should only be temporary. The mirror dimension itself does not appear to be inherently unstable. It is - generally - as stable as our own reality.

Scientists in the Indiana lab who attempted to study the Nether in 1983 did not report any incidents of earthquakes - though admittedly their exploration of this shadow realm was limited to say the least and also constricted by their focus on recovering test subject 011. If you detect any ground tremors in the Nether do not attempt to travel as normal because you may well lose your footing and get injured. Use plain old common sense in situations like this. If you think a situation is hazardous (and a mild earthquake definitely could be construed as hazardous) then wait for the tremors to pass before you attempt to make any further progress on foot.

The same is true of electrical storms in the mirror world. If the storms seem especially obstreperous then seek cover in a lightning strobed scenario like this. You should be able to keep moving during a storm under the cover of trees or buildings but stay alert to any danger. Lightning seems to be far more common in the Nether than our world so don't get spooked if you experience of a lot of this phenomena. Lightning just seems to be a natural part of this dimension and will occur many times. For the record, no survivors from Nether trips have reported that mirror dimension lightning was ever a problem or obvious danger. No one from our dimension has ever been struck by lightning in the Nether.

One salient question concerning Nether creatures is the matter of how they smell. Do they give off a palpable odour? This is important because if a smell gives Nether creatures away then this would give one the ability to know that a Demogorgon is near - even if you have yet to sight the creature. Sadly though, there have been no reports by anyone (whether a civilian, scientist, or soldier) of Demogorgons radiating a particular smell in any strength. They seem to be strangely neutral in this regard. As for the Nether, scientists who have experienced this ruined void - they did so with hazmat suits so were unaware of any native smells. Civilians who have survived the Nether have not reported any particular odour though one would imagine it didn't smell of roses.

One would expect the Nether to smell something akin to a giant garbage tip but this patently isn't the case. Though the Nether is decayed the lack of human pollution renders it more neutral than you might expect when it comes to odours. I need hardly remind the reader that our own dimension is far from perfect. We have polluted the air, oceans, and rivers with waste, chemicals, and the by products of industry. A Demogorgon might even consider our realm to be rather smelly - even in comparison to the mist laden nightmare world from whence it came.

Smell will probably not save your life then but noise might. Listen for the clicking sound of a lurking Demogorgon. Those who have experienced an encounter with DemoDogs report that they emit a sort of babbling growl - like some unearthly hybrid of dog and sheep. This may or may not be accurate but it might be worth remembering all the same in case there is any veracity in this observation. While we have stressed that fighting a Demogorgon in a one on one situation is a futile and suicidal scenario, there are conflicting reports when it comes to DemoDogs. Though powerful, DemoDogs are considerably smaller than Demogorgons and it may be the case that with a reliable weapon (something like a baseball bat for example) you may be able to fend one off. This is most assuredly not the case with a herd of DemoDogs though. In this situation you would simply be overwhelmed.

It is understandable that it may be difficult for some people to get guns during a Nether crisis. If you reside in a nation that has no gun culture then guns are exceptionally difficult to get hold of. There are many nations in the world with strict gun laws and no gun stores. If you live in the United Kingdom for example you could feasibly go through your whole life without ever seeing a real gun let alone actually use one. This is not necessarily the end of the world though because as we have noted throughout this document on Nether scenarios there is ample evidence that guns are not (to risk a bad pun again) a magic bullet solution against the creatures of the Upside Down.

For reasons we have already discussed, having a basic handgun is probably not going to save you from a rampaging Demogorgon. If one can not get hold of guns it is worth trying a bow and arrow as an alternative weapon. While a simple arrow is not going to kill a Demogorgon it will distract the monster. Most importantly of all, an arrow can be wrapped in bandages and a flammable liquid and set alight before it is shot at the Demogorgon. This type of tactic could be very effective. Arrows can also be used as misdirection if you are being stalked by a Demogorgon.

If you can get hold of a good bow and arrow this could be a useful weapon indeed in a Nether crisis. Make sure though that you or anyone else using a bow and arrow is proficient with the weapon and have plenty of practice. There is not much point in having a bow and arrow if your arrows miss the target all the time and you are useless at using the bow.

If you research bow and arrows there is plenty of information on how you can fashion one yourself from wood but you are better advised to simply purchase one because the bow is likely to be more durable and reliable than one you have made yourself.

There are conflicting reports on the safety of the surface in the Upside Down. Few have spoken at any length about the conditions inside the Nether because few have been in this dimension and of those that did experience the Upside Down the majority perished and few of the survivors ever spoke about what they found there. It is understandable that civilian survivors of a Nether crisis were not in a rush to broadcast tales of alternate dimensions and monsters because people would simply think they were mad. There would also be the not insignificant problem either of the respective government. A civilian who spoke of the Nether would be regarded as a 'whistle blower' by the authorities and we've seen what happens to whistle blowers. They tend to end up behind bars - often for a very long time.

There are no reports of any bog or quicksand type regions in the Nether but given that this dimension is a parallel (albeit a topsy turvy nightmare parallel) of our own world it seems logical to presume that there must be boggy and dangerous areas like this. You must always expect the unexpected in the Nether dimension. If you find yourself inside the Nether you must of course tread lightly and make sure you do not walk over any ground in which you might potentially sink. If you were trapped in Upside Down quicksand your situation would be completely hopeless.

EagleCreek.Com offers the following tips for those trapped in quicksand - ' Eliminate excess weight: Throw your backpack to the side, and take off your shoes, if possible. The lighter you can make your body, the easier it will be to extract yourself. Backpedal: Before you sink too deep, take a few quick steps backward to where the ground was solid. Avoid large lunging steps, because a straddled position will make it harder to manoeuvrer if one leg gets stuck. Head Above Water: Keep your arms and head above the surface at all times.

'Float Your Way Out: If you sink and find yourself waist deep, lean back into a back float position. Much like sitting, this evenly distributes your weight, and allows your feet to float up to the surface. After your feet break through the surface, slowly inch your way to "shore." Use Your Resources: Assess your surroundings, and utilize any trees with reachable branches. Only grab them after you have achieved a safe position (back float or seated with legs above surface). Free Your Legs: Inch by inch, move your legs one at a time upward toward the surface of the quicksand. With every inch you move a leg up, allow a moment for the quicksand to fill the space it once occupied.

'Depending on how deep you have sunk, this process could take hours. Patience will prevail, while big movements will further liquefy the quicksand and reverse your progress. Use a Trekking Pole: If you have a trekking pole with you, now is the time to use it (arguably it was before you got stuck, but hindsight is 20/20!). Lay the pole on the surface of the quicksand, and lower your back onto it. This will help stabilize you while freeing your legs. Breathe Deeply: This will promote both buoyancy and calmness.'

There isn't much background noise in the Nether compared to our dimension. There is no traffic, no chatter of human voices, no birdsong, no music, no planes in the sky. The relative quiet (save for the ominous noise of distant creatures) of the Nether should work to your advantage and enable you to listen carefully for any predators that may be lurking in the mist. DemoBats tend to announce their arrival with a high pitched screech and as such you should be able to detect them long before they actually reach you. Be warned though that by all accounts (which are admittedly few) these bats are very fast and so will upon you much quicker you might have expected.

Factor this into your strategy should you end up in the Nether and encounter dimensional bats. Run for cover as soon as you hear a screech. Do not idle around in open ground and make yourself a tempting target.

If you find guns in the Nether there is probably no reason why they shouldn't still work - so long as they have been stored in a dry place out of the elements. If you live in the United States or a nation where police officers are well armed then a police station in the Nether is likely to contain many firearms and much ammunition and would be a good place to search for guns so long as it isn't too far away from your location. Do not get too distracted though by a search for guns. Your main focus should be on locating a dimensional portal. Only search a building for guns if it falls fairly directly on the route you were taking and you deem the building to be safe.

It stands to reason that the more powerful the gun the more use it will be in a Nether crisis. Once again we must stress that you must not allow guns to give you a false sense of security. Stealth and silence will be far more valuable weapons in the Nether than the ability to shoot a gun. It might be advisable to invest in some light sticks or glow sticks during a Nether crisis. These are small luminous sticks which will (as the name suggests) create light in an emergency. They can also be used as markers or might even serve as something which may distract a Nether creature if thrown as misdirection.

These light sticks can be quite expensive so you might need to club together with others to purchase some. Be careful with your use of illumination inside the Nether. If you walk around with a flashlight constantly on you might attract unwanted attention and give your location away. Though meat can be used as way to lure a DemoDog into a trap, it is not recommended that you carry meat around with you because this will merely attract the attention of any Nether creature - most notably a Demogorgon- that may be in the vicinity. You must always make sure that your smell remains neutral and that you don't stand out during a Nether crisis.

It is not recommended that you attempt to use pepper spray on a Demogorgon because there is no evidence to suggest it would have any effect. Even if you were to use the spray in the unfurled fanged mouth of the creature (which MIGHT have at least some effect) by this stage it would probably be too late because the creature would be in close proximity. Some pepper spray would be unlikely to stop the creature from now chomping down on your head at such close range.

In a desperate last resort situation there are everyday things you could try and use as a weapon on a Nether creature. It depends on what you have to hand. A cricket bat, baseball bat, hammer, scissors, dumbbell, shovel. Some of these will weapons will obviously be more effective than others. It is doubtful that trying to snare a Demogorgon in a net is a viable strategy because the creature is so strong and powerful it will simply break free of the net. Trapping a Demogorgon in a net might buy you a few extra seconds but that's about it. A trap or setting the creature on fire would be more effective if you wanted to stop the creature long enough to escape.

Fireworks may be of use during a Nether crisis. They can be used for misdirection and if fired directly at a Nether creature may stop its forward momentum and distract or hurt the creature sufficiently to aid you in a crisis. There are vague unverified reports that fireworks proved quite effective against a Flayer monster in 1985 when the creature went on a rampage at a shopping mall. Demogorgons are tough and implacable but no creature - from whatever dimension - is going to like having fireworks set off in their direction - let alone their head.

An incendiary device (aka smoke bomb) may also be of assistance if one wishes to escape from a lurking Demogorgon. The smoke will provide valuable cover and stealth. You must make sure though that in such a scenario you don't lose your bearings and walk straight into the path of the monster through the haze. A spear may be of use during a Nether crisis because it would provide a means to defend oneself against a Denogorgon and ward the creature off at close range. Make sure the spear is lightweight though because you don't want to be carrying around anything that is too heavy and so might restrict your ability to move quickly. A spear would provide you with a means to mitigate the huge reach advantage a Demogorgon will enjoy over humans.

While a spear is unlikely to kill a Demogorgon it can be jabbed at the creature as a last resort to keep it at bay long enough for assistance to arrive or it may give you enough breathing space to dive for a prepared exit. You can fashion an improvised spear from wood if you don't have one to hand. You'll obviously need time to do this though so make sure you do this during a peaceful period. With bandages and a flammable liquid you can also turn a spear into a flaming torch.

A spear that has fire at the tip would be an invaluable weapon against a Demogorgon and most likely much more effective against the monster than a handgun. If you find yourself having to face a Demogorgon an obvious but vital tip is to keep moving. Do not present a stationary target. Your main objective will be to avoid the deadly rakes of the creature's claws. Ideally you will need something sharp or preferably aflame to keep the creature at bay. Fire will make the creature hesitate. This is crucial because the creature will no longer be reckless and fast. It will be cautious - a quality not usually associated with this instinctive foe.

You should be reminded that a bandana is an excellent accessory in a Nether crisis because it can be used used as a makeshift face covering and also as a tourniquet for bandaging a wound. Remember to always have water with you in case you end up trapped in the Nether. Humans can only survive a few days without water. You may find a source of water in the Nether but you are advised not to drink it as the chances of it being safe are minimal. If you have a bandana in can be used as a very rudimentary water filter in an extreme emergency.

You may potentially find yourself in a grim situation where you have no option but to drink water found in the Nether. Water purifying tablets may be of some assistance in the Nether if you are desperate for water and can only find a muddied source in the Nether but you should only drink any Nether water as an absolute last resort. There isn't much evidence of water in the Nether anyway so you don't really want to end up in a situation where you are searching for water in the Upside Down.

As for whether or not a Nether parallel of a store would contain canned drinks, well, we simply, don't know. No one has ever reported anything like this. It is not something you should count on. The best thing is to make sure you have your own bottles of clean water and ration them as parsimoniously as you can. A garbage bag or bin liner might be a useful item to have on you in a Nether scenario because it is lightweight to carry and if you cut a hole in the top and put it on it will help to keep you warm and dry. It will be chilly inside the Nether so anything that will keep you warmer in valuable.

A garbage bag will also be much less likely to attract Nether dust and debris than normal clothes. Duct tape is another excellent accessory to have during a Nether crisis because it can be used as a makeshift bandage. Duct tape can also be used to put on any blisters that have formed through walking too much on rough terrain. If you are trapped in the Upside Down and wish to communicate with colleagues on the other side with lights make sure that you all know the SOS signal. An SOS signal would be three short bursts of light followed by three long bursts followed by three more short bursts.

Though communication through lights is not easy it is at least possible. If you become trapped in the Nether comfort yourself with the knowledge that you are not completely cut off from your friends and colleagues in our own dimension. There is a way to let them know you are ok - but merely trapped in the mirror dimension. You can use the lights as a signal to let them know that you need assistance.

If you are dealing with the Nether entity known as Vecna then it is important to remember that the murder sites related to this antagonist tend to leave dimensional portals in their wake. This is potentially very significant because if you are trapped in the Nether and know of a place where someone was killed by this entity in our reality then the Upside Down version of that location may well still contain a dimensional rip that will enable you to get back to our own world. Move with all haste though because we simply don't know how long these 'rips' stay open until they begin to heal and close again.

If your knife seems to be blunt in the Nether you should be able to sharpen it on a rock. Make sure though that you don't make too much noise when doing this. A fold-up knife is logical to carry because it will take up less room among your possessions. A good reliable lighter is essential to carry on you during a Nether crisis and make sure you have some flammable liquid too. Alcohol will serve this purpose but, as we noted earlier, you should not be tempted to drink any alcohol while in the Nether because you need to stay sharp and have crystal clarity. The only time you might conceivably flout this rule is if either you or someone with you is injured or suffering from shock. A nip of alcohol for medicinal purposes may be sensible in this scenario.

The important thing to remember is that even if you vanquish an Upside Down threat you never know when the next dimensional crisis will emerge. It could be months later or years later. The Mind Flayer in particular will not simply give up on invading our dimension. It will patiently wait until the next opportunity arises. Though we know little about the Flayer it would safe to presume that this is an ancient entity who has a different conception of time from us. The events of 1983 and 1984 and 1985 are a mere millisecond ago to the Mind Flayer.

It is impossible to know if the Flayer is ever defeated for good. All you can do is banish the threat for now and be on the look out for strange goings on in your town. Rotted crops, baffling murders, people who don't seem to be acting like themselves anymore. Things like this could be clues that a dimensional crisis is heading your way. The most important thing in any dimensional crisis is to remain calm. Concentrate on the task in hand and focus on the positives rather than the negatives. Remember that several civilians have battled the Nether creatures, visited the Upside Down, and survived all of these challenges. If you have the right equipment, trusted allies, and the right strategies for specific situations there is no reason why you can't do the same.